2020 Planner

2020 Planner

*A years guide to time
management and work life
balance in social care*

Melissa Pearl

Library of Congress Control Number: 2018913494
ISBN: Hardcover   978-1-5434-9333-7
               Softcover   978-1-5434-9334-4
               eBook   978-1-5434-9332-0

Print information available on the last page.

Rev. date: 12/12/2018

To order additional copies of this book, contact:
Xlibris
800-056-3182
www.Xlibrispublishing.co.uk
Orders@Xlibrispublishing.co.uk
786802

This planner belongs to

....

2020

Personal Info

Address: _____

Email Address: _____

Telephone Number: _____

Fax: _____

2020 at a Glance

January 2020

Sun	Mon	Tue	Wed	Thu	Fri	Sat
			1	2	3	4
5	6	7	8	9	10	11
12	13	14	15	16	17	18
19	20	21	22	23	24	25
26	27	28	29	30	31	

February 2020

Sun	Mon	Tue	Wed	Thu	Fri	Sat
						1
2	3	4	5	6	7	8
9	10	11	12	13	14	15
16	17	18	19	20	21	22
23	24	25	26	27	28	29

March 2020

Sun	Mon	Tue	Wed	Thu	Fri	Sat
1	2	3	4	5	6	7
8	9	10	11	12	13	14
15	16	17	18	19	20	21
22	23	24	25	26	27	28
29	30	31				

2020 at a Glance

April 2020

Sun	Mon	Tue	Wed	Thu	Fri	Sat
			1	2	3	4
5	6	7	8	9	10	11
12	13	14	15	16	17	18
19	20	21	22	23	24	25
26	27	28	29	30		

May 2020

Sun	Mon	Tue	Wed	Thu	Fri	Sat
					1	2
3	4	5	6	7	8	9
10	11	12	13	14	15	16
17	18	19	20	21	22	23
24	25	26	27	28	29	30
31						

June 2020

Sun	Mon	Tue	Wed	Thu	Fri	Sat
	1	2	3	4	5	6
7	8	9	10	11	12	13
14	15	16	17	18	19	20
21	22	23	24	25	26	27
28	29	30				

2020 at a Glance

July 2020

Sun	Mon	Tue	Wed	Thu	Fri	Sat
			1	2	3	4
5	6	7	8	9	10	11
12	13	14	15	16	17	18
19	20	21	22	23	24	25
26	27	28	29	30	31	

August 2020

Sun	Mon	Tue	Wed	Thu	Fri	Sat
						1
2	3	4	5	6	7	8
9	10	11	12	13	14	15
16	17	18	19	20	21	22
23	24	25	26	27	28	29
30	31					

September 2020

Sun	Mon	Tue	Wed	Thu	Fri	Sat
		1	2	3	4	5
6	7	8	9	10	11	12
13	14	15	16	17	18	19
20	21	22	23	24	25	26
27	28	29	30			

2020 at a Glance

October 2020

Sun	Mon	Tue	Wed	Thu	Fri	Sat
				1	2	3
4	5	6	7	8	9	10
11	12	13	14	15	16	17
18	19	20	21	22	23	24
25	26	27	28	29	30	31

November 2020

Sun	Mon	Tue	Wed	Thu	Fri	Sat
1	2	3	4	5	6	7
8	9	10	11	12	13	14
15	16	17	18	19	20	21
22	23	24	25	26	27	28
29	30					

December 2020

Sun	Mon	Tue	Wed	Thu	Fri	Sat
		1	2	3	4	5
6	7	8	9	10	11	12
13	14	15	16	17	18	19
20	21	22	23	24	25	26
27	28	29	30	31		

One day at a time,
one goal at a time.
Make it happen for *you*.

Weekly Goal

List the top 3 goals you want to achieve this week:

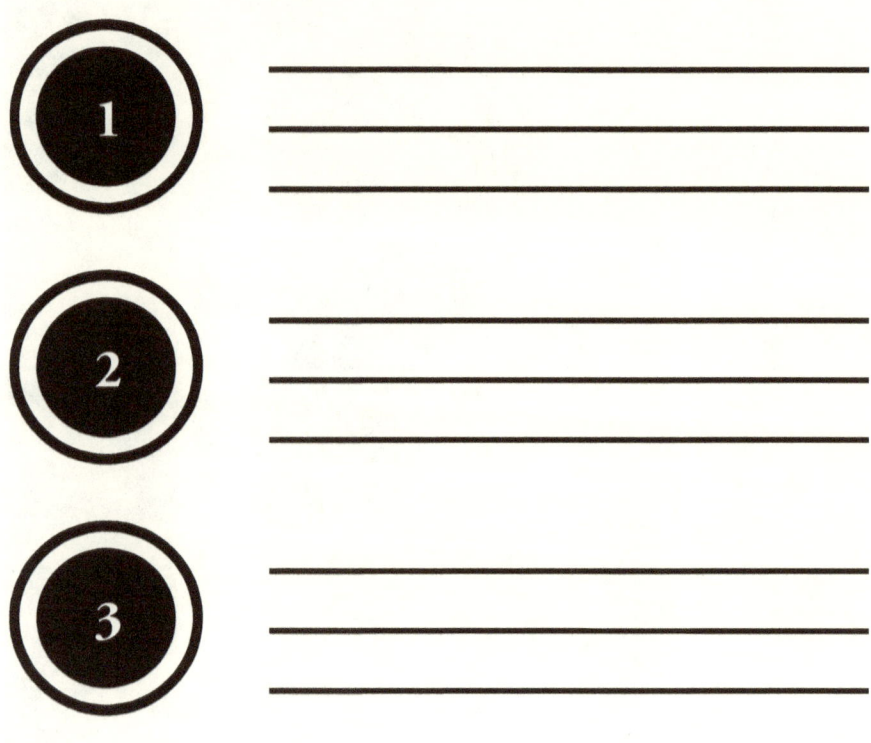

1 _____

_____

_____

2 _____

_____

_____

3 _____

_____

_____

What do you need to do in order to achieve your goals?

_____

_____

_____

Me time: what will you do for *you* this week?

January
2020

January 2020
Su	M	Tu	W	Th	F	Sa
			1	2	3	4
5	6	7	8	9	10	11
12	13	14	15	16	17	18
19	20	21	22	23	24	25
26	27	28	29	30	31	

MON	
TUE	
WED 01	
THUR 02	
FRI 03	
SAT 04	
SUN 05	

9

Checklist:

                                                    ☐

_____

    ☐

_____

    ☐

_____

    ☐

_____

    ☐

_____

    ☐

_____

Notes:

_____
_____
_____

Reflections

What happened this week, and what did you learn?

This is your week.
Challenge yourself to work
within your set target
to achieve a work/life
balance.

Weekly Goal

List the top 3 goals you want to achieve this week:

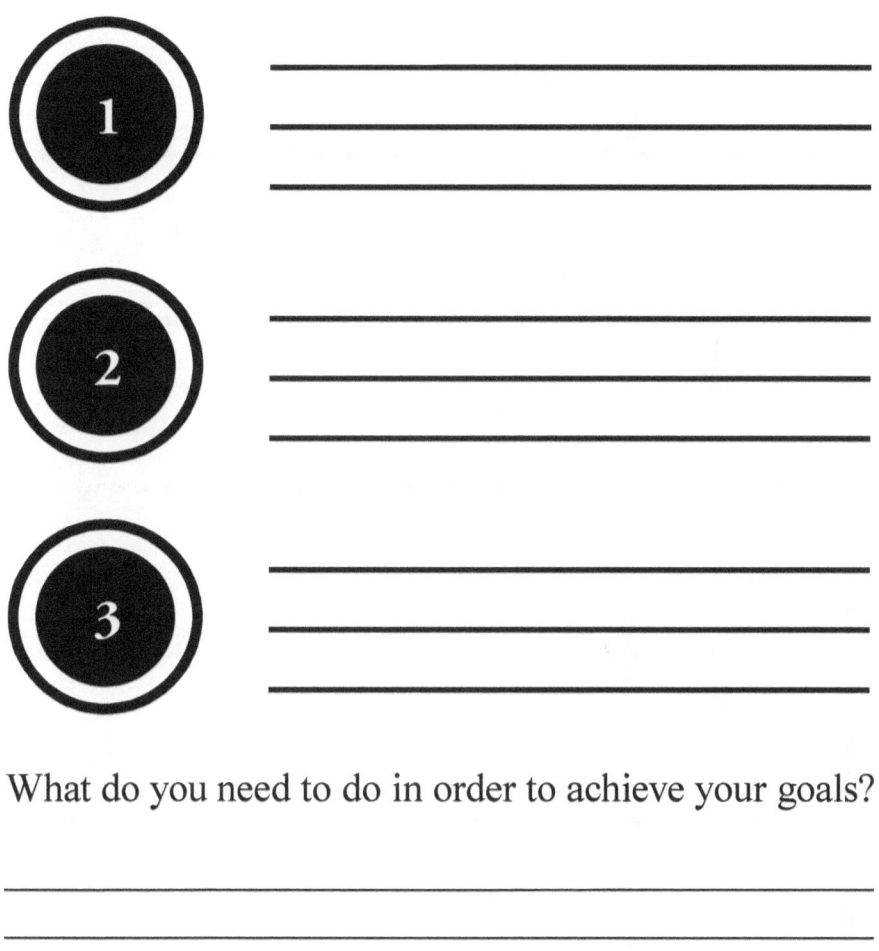

1 _____
_____
_____

2 _____
_____
_____

3 _____
_____
_____

What do you need to do in order to achieve your goals?

_____
_____
_____

Me time: what will you do for *you* this week?

January
2020

January 2020

Su	M	Tu	W	Th	F	Sa
			1	2	3	4
5	6	7	8	9	10	11
12	13	14	15	16	17	18
19	20	21	22	23	24	25
26	27	28	29	30	31	

MON 06	
TUE 07	
WED 08	
THUR 09	
FRI 10	
SAT 11	
SUN 12	

Checklist:

_____ ☐

_____ ☐

_____ ☐

_____ ☐

_____ ☐

_____ ☐

Notes:

_____

_____

_____

Reflections

What happened this week, and what did you learn?

No matter how tough the
day can become, remember
you are well able and
can overcome.

Weekly Goal

List the top 3 goals you want to achieve this week:

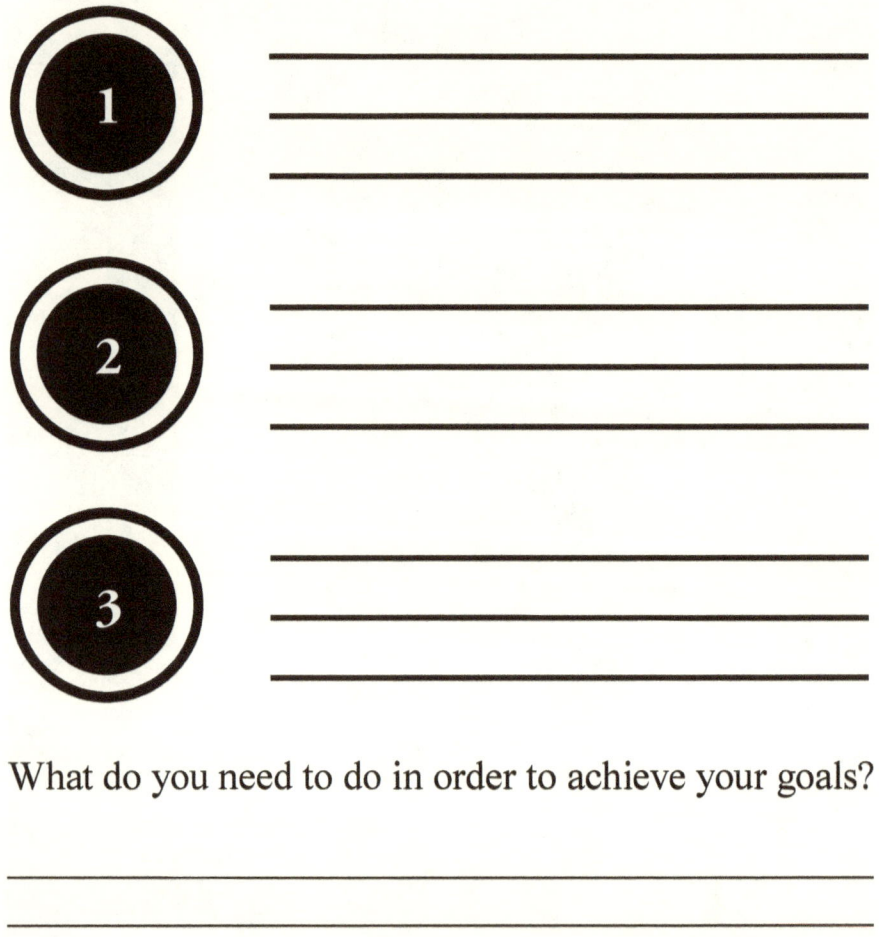

1 _____
_____
_____

2 _____
_____
_____

3 _____
_____
_____

What do you need to do in order to achieve your goals?

_____
_____
_____

Me time: what will you do for *you* this week?

January
2020

January 2020
Su	M	Tu	W	Th	F	Sa
			1	2	3	4
5	6	7	8	9	10	11
12	13	14	15	16	17	18
19	20	21	22	23	24	25
26	27	28	29	30	31	

MON 13	
TUE 14	
WED 15	
THUR 16	
FRI 17	
SAT 18	
SUN 19	

Checklist:

_____ ☐

_____ ☐

_____ ☐

_____ ☐

_____ ☐

_____ ☐

Notes:

_____

_____

_____

Reflections

What happened this week, and what did you learn?

Take charge of your week.

Weekly Goal

List the top 3 goals you want to achieve this week:

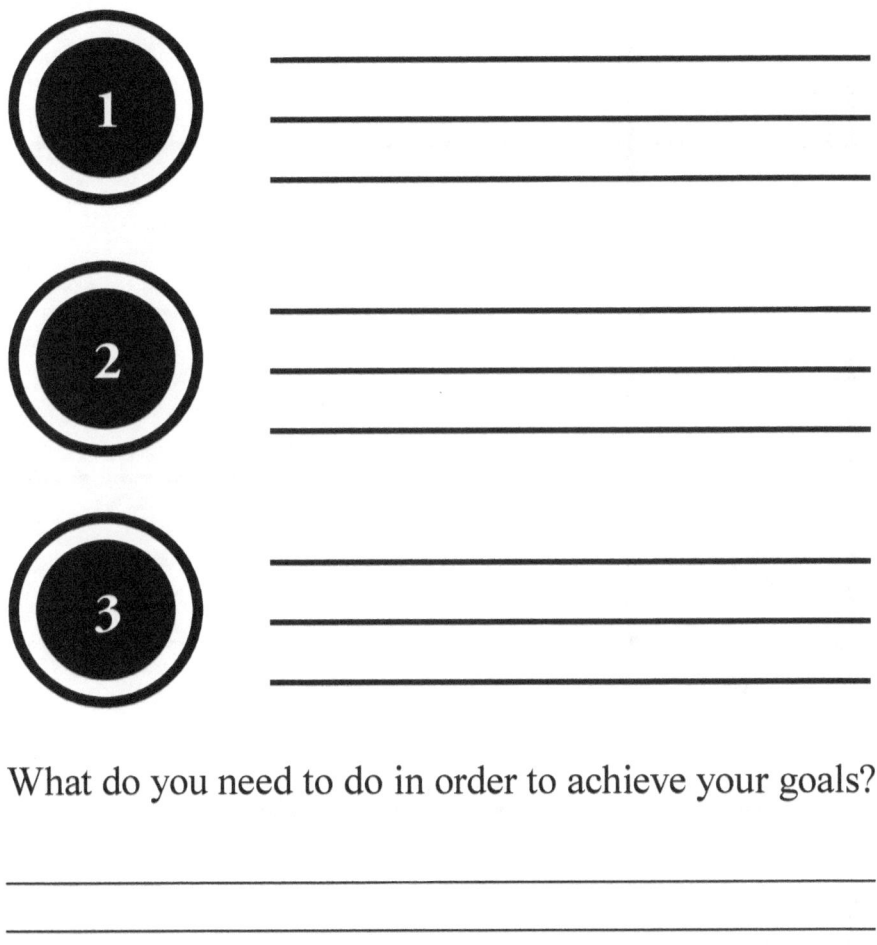

1 _____
_____
_____

2 _____
_____
_____

3 _____
_____
_____

What do you need to do in order to achieve your goals?

_____
_____
_____

Me time: what will you do for _you_ this week?

January
2020

January 2020

Su	M	Tu	W	Th	F	Sa
			1	2	3	4
5	6	7	8	9	10	11
12	13	14	15	16	17	18
19	20	21	22	23	24	25
26	27	28	29	30	31	

MON 20	
TUE 21	
WED 22	
THUR 23	
FRI 24	
SAT 25	
SUN 26	

Checklist:

_____ ☐

_____ ☐

_____ ☐

_____ ☐

_____ ☐

_____ ☐

Notes:

_____

_____

_____

Reflections

What happened this week, and what did you learn?

You are great at
what you do. It's time
you believe it.

Weekly Goal

List the top 3 goals you want to achieve this week:

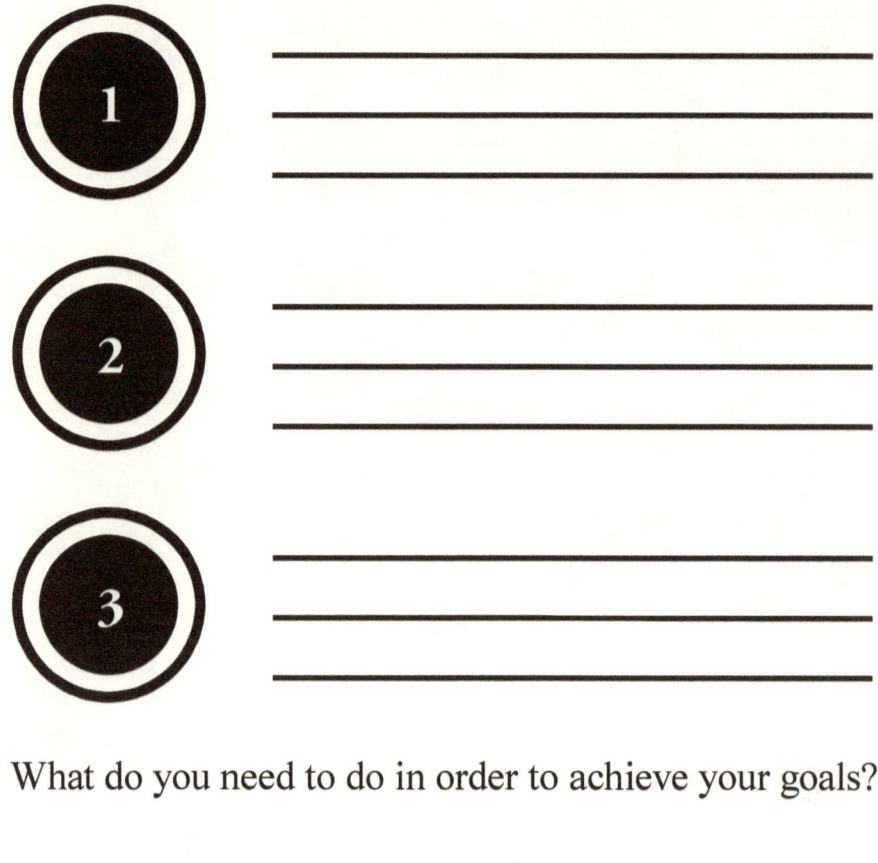

1 _____

_____

_____

2 _____

_____

_____

3 _____

_____

_____

What do you need to do in order to achieve your goals?

_____

_____

_____

Me time: what will you do for *you* this week?

January
2020

January 2020

Su	M	Tu	W	Th	F	Sa
			1	2	3	4
5	6	7	8	9	10	11
12	13	14	15	16	17	18
19	20	21	22	23	24	25
26	27	28	29	30	31	

MON 27	
TUE 28	
WED 29	
THUR 30	
FRI 31	
SAT 01	
SUN 02	

Checklist:

_____ ☐

_____ ☐

_____ ☐

_____ ☐

_____ ☐

_____ ☐

Notes:

_____

_____

_____

Reflections

What happened this week, and what did you learn?

Emails are instant, but
that does not mean your
response has to be.
Stop and think before
you reply.

Weekly Goal

List the top 3 goals you want to achieve this week:

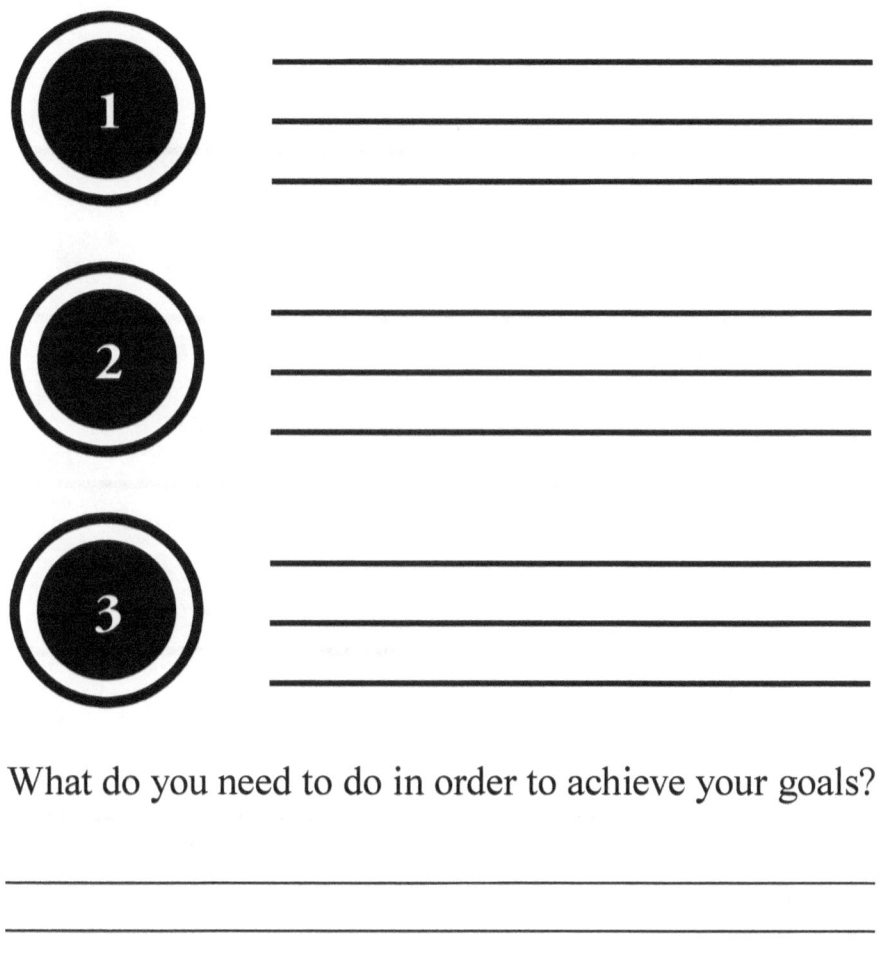

1 _____
_____
_____

2 _____
_____
_____

3 _____
_____

What do you need to do in order to achieve your goals?

_____
_____
_____

Me time: what will you do for *you* this week?

February
2020

February 2020

Su	M	Tu	W	Th	F	Sa
						1
2	3	4	5	6	7	8
9	10	11	12	13	14	15
16	17	18	19	20	21	22
23	24	25	26	27	28	29

MON 03	
TUE 04	
WED 05	
THUR 06	
FRI 07	
SAT 08	
SUN 09	

Checklist:

_____	☐
_____	☐
_____	☐
_____	☐
_____	☐
_____	☐

Notes:

_____

_____

_____

Reflections

What happened this week, and what did you learn?

If it can wait until
tomorrow or next week,
it is OK. Always
remember to prioritise.

Weekly Goal

List the top 3 goals you want to achieve this week:

1 _____
_____
_____

2 _____
_____
_____

3 _____
_____
_____

What do you need to do in order to achieve your goals?

_____
_____
_____

Me time: what will you do for *you* this week?

February
2020

February 2020

Su	M	Tu	W	Th	F	Sa
						1
2	3	4	5	6	7	8
9	10	11	12	13	14	15
16	17	18	19	20	21	22
23	24	25	26	27	28	29

MON 10	
TUE 11	
WED 12	
THUR 13	
FRI 14	
SAT 15	
SUN 16	

Checklist:

_____ □

_____ □

_____ □

_____ □

_____ □

_____ □

Notes:

_____

_____

_____

Reflections

What happened this week, and what did you learn?

Take a moment to feel
that emotion, inhale,
and exhale before
you move on to the
next task or goal.

Weekly Goal

List the top 3 goals you want to achieve this week:

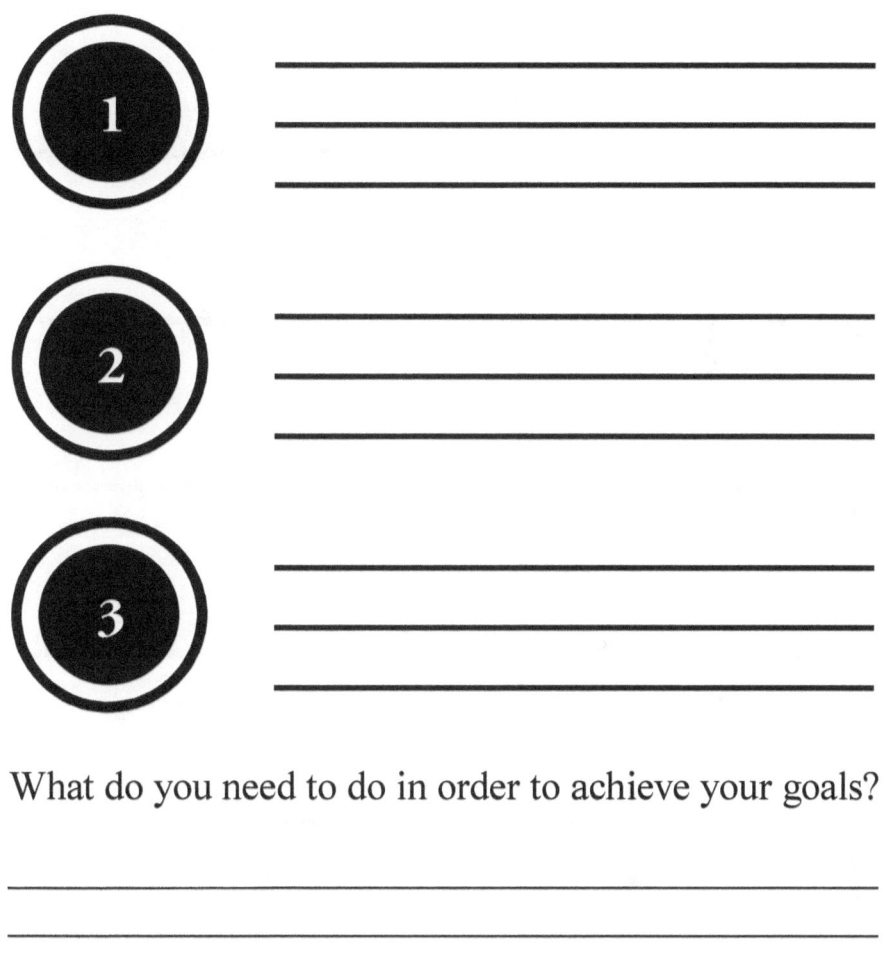

1 _____

_____

_____

2 _____

_____

_____

3 _____

_____

_____

What do you need to do in order to achieve your goals?

_____

_____

_____

Me time: what will you do for *you* this week?

February
2020

February 2020

Su	M	Tu	W	Th	F	Sa
						1
2	3	4	5	6	7	8
9	10	11	12	13	14	15
16	17	18	19	20	21	22
23	24	25	26	27	28	29

MON 17	
TUE 18	
WED 19	
THUR 20	
FRI 21	
SAT 22	
SUN 23	

Checklist:

_____ ☐

_____ ☐

_____ ☐

_____ ☐

_____ ☐

_____ ☐

Notes:

_____

_____

_____

Reflections

What happened this week, and what did you learn?

Do you remember your
first day on the job?
Look at how far
you have come.

Weekly Goal

List the top 3 goals you want to achieve this week:

What do you need to do in order to achieve your goals?

_____

_____

_____

Me time: what will you do for *you* this week?

February
2020

February 2020						
Su	M	Tu	W	Th	F	Sa
						1
2	3	4	5	6	7	8
9	10	11	12	13	14	15
16	17	18	19	20	21	22
23	24	25	26	27	28	29

MON 24	
TUE 25	
WED 26	
THUR 27	
FRI 28	
SAT 29	
SUN 01	

Checklist:

_____ ☐

_____ ☐

_____ ☐

_____ ☐

_____ ☐

_____ ☐

Notes:

_____

_____

_____

Reflections

What happened this week, and what did you learn?

Let this week be
innovative
and productive.

Weekly Goal

List the top 3 goals you want to achieve this week:

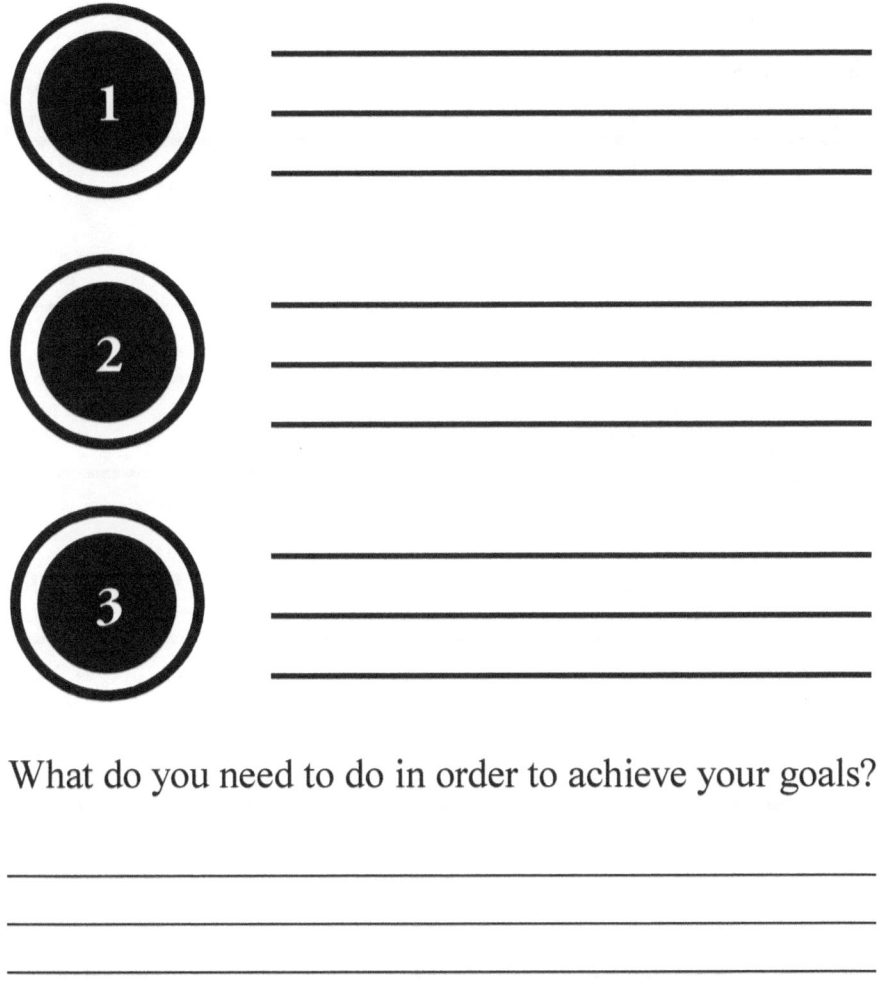

What do you need to do in order to achieve your goals?

Me time: what will you do for *you* this week?

March
2020

March 2020

Su	M	Tu	W	Th	F	Sa
1	2	3	4	5	6	7
8	9	10	11	12	13	14
15	16	17	18	19	20	21
22	23	24	25	26	27	28
29	30	31				

MON 02	
TUE 03	
WED 04	
THUR 05	
FRI 06	
SAT 07	
SUN 08	

Checklist:

_____ ☐

_____ ☐

_____ ☐

_____ ☐

_____ ☐

_____ ☐

Notes:

_____

_____

_____

Reflections

What happened this week, and what did you learn?

You are valuable.
You have made
a difference.

Weekly Goal

List the top 3 goals you want to achieve this week:

1 _____
_____
_____

2 _____
_____
_____

3 _____
_____
_____

What do you need to do in order to achieve your goals?

_____
_____
_____

Me time: what will you do for *you* this week?

March
2020

March 2020

Su	M	Tu	W	Th	F	Sa
1	2	3	4	5	6	7
8	9	10	11	12	13	14
15	16	17	18	19	20	21
22	23	24	25	26	27	28
29	30	31				

MON 09	
TUE 10	
WED 11	
THUR 12	
FRI 13	
SAT 14	
SUN 15	

Checklist:

_____ ☐

_____ ☐

_____ ☐

_____ ☐

_____ ☐

_____ ☐

Notes:

_____

_____

_____

Reflections

What happened this week, and what did you learn?

Your health comes first.
When you take care of
yourself, you can take
care of others.

Weekly Goal

List the top 3 goals you want to achieve this week:

What do you need to do in order to achieve your goals?

_____

_____

_____

Me time: what will you do for *you* this week?

March
2020

March 2020

Su	M	Tu	W	Th	F	Sa
1	2	3	4	5	6	7
8	9	10	11	12	13	14
15	16	17	18	19	20	21
22	23	24	25	26	27	28
29	30	31				

MON 16	
TUE 17	
WED 18	
THUR 19	
FRI 20	
SAT 21	
SUN 22	

Checklist:

_____ ☐

_____ ☐

_____ ☐

_____ ☐

_____ ☐

_____ ☐

Notes:

_____

_____

_____

Reflections

What happened this week, and what did you learn?

When was the last time
you did something for you?
Nothing is wrong with
scheduling some time
for yourself.

Weekly Goal

List the top 3 goals you want to achieve this week:

1 _____
_____
_____

2 _____
_____
_____

3 _____
_____
_____

What do you need to do in order to achieve your goals?

_____
_____
_____

Me time: what will you do for *you* this week?

March
2020

March 2020

Su	M	Tu	W	Th	F	Sa
1	2	3	4	5	6	7
8	9	10	11	12	13	14
15	16	17	18	19	20	21
22	23	24	25	26	27	28
29	30	31				

MON 23	
TUE 24	
WED 25	
THUR 26	
FRI 27	
SAT 28	
SUN 29	

Checklist:

_____ ☐

_____ ☐

_____ ☐

_____ ☐

_____ ☐

_____ ☐

Notes:

_____

_____

_____

Reflections

What happened this week, and what did you learn?

Always remember not to work in isolation. Talk with others, and share ideas for a better outcome.

Weekly Goal

List the top 3 goals you want to achieve this week:

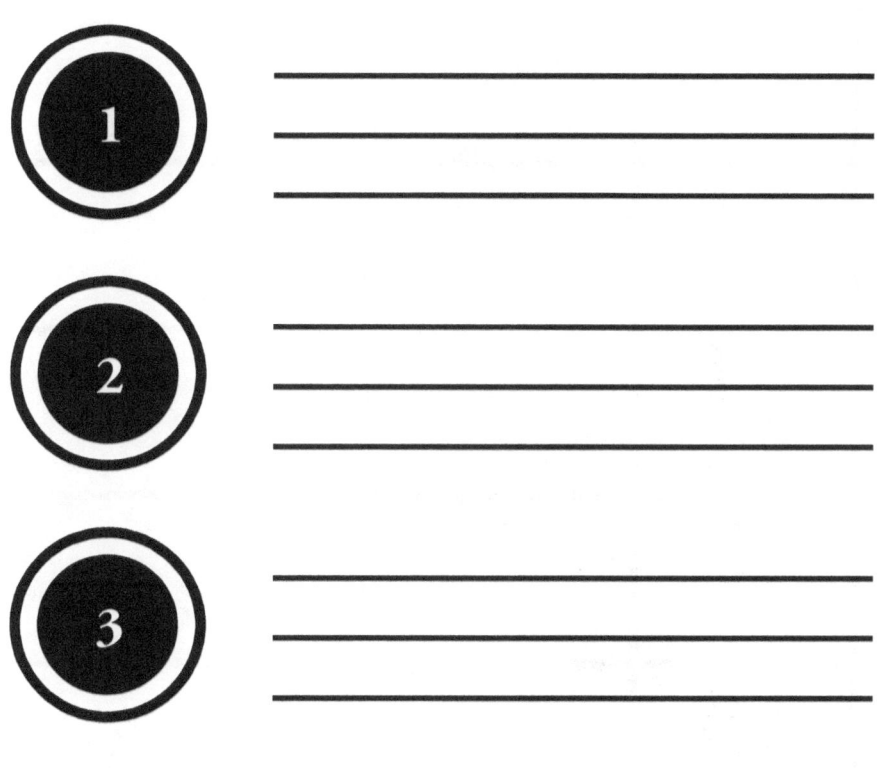

1 _____
_____
_____

2 _____
_____
_____

3 _____
_____

What do you need to do in order to achieve your goals?

_____
_____
_____

Me time: what will you do for *you* this week?

April
2020

April 2020

Su	M	Tu	W	Th	F	Sa
			1	2	3	4
5	6	7	8	9	10	11
12	13	14	15	16	17	18
19	20	21	22	23	24	25
26	27	28	29	30		

MON 30	
TUE 31	
WED 01	
THUR 02	
FRI 03	
SAT 04	
SUN 05	

Checklist:

_____ ☐

_____ ☐

_____ ☐

_____ ☐

_____ ☐

_____ ☐

Notes:

_____

_____

_____

Reflections

What happened this week, and what did you learn?

You are an asset to the
community. Have a
great week.

Weekly Goal

List the top 3 goals you want to achieve this week:

What do you need to do in order to achieve your goals?

_____

_____

_____

Me time: what will you do for *you* this week?

April
2020

April 2020

Su	M	Tu	W	Th	F	Sa
			1	2	3	4
5	6	7	8	9	10	11
12	13	14	15	16	17	18
19	20	21	22	23	24	25
26	27	28	29	30		

MON 06	
TUE 07	
WED 08	
THUR 09	
FRI 10	
SAT 11	
SUN 12	

Checklist:

_____ ☐

_____ ☐

_____ ☐

_____ ☐

_____ ☐

_____ ☐

Notes:

_____

_____

_____

Reflections

What happened this week, and what did you learn?

You can do it.
Keep going.

Weekly Goal

List the top 3 goals you want to achieve this week:

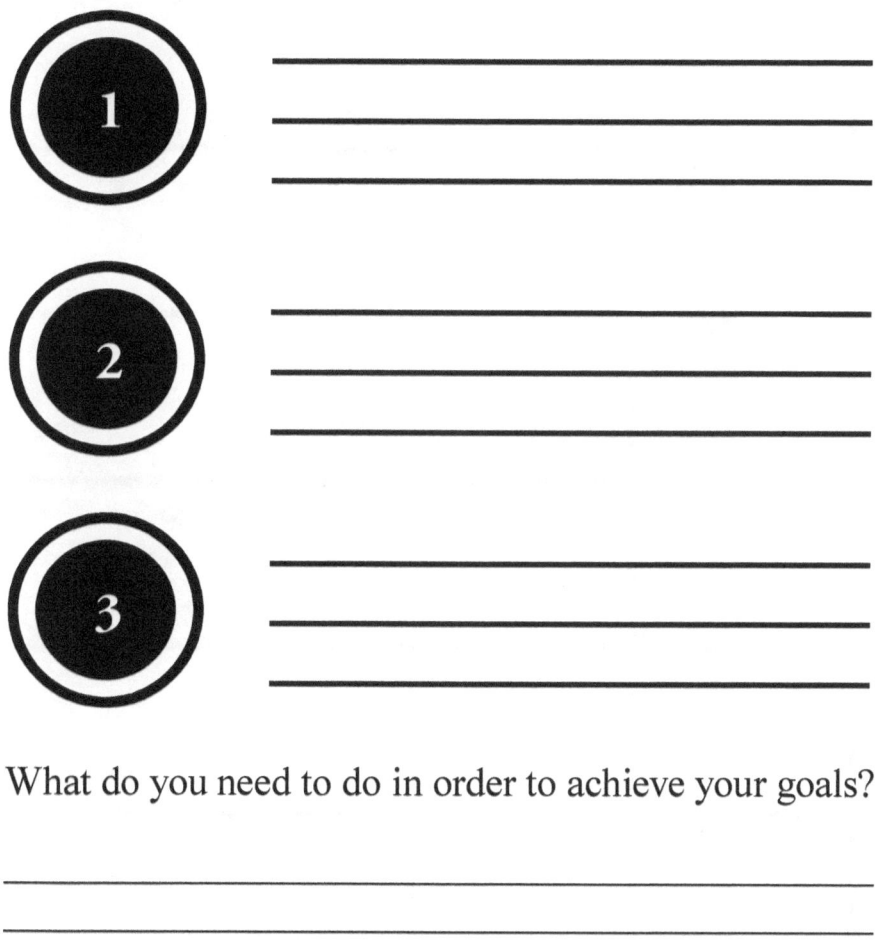

1 _____

_____

_____

2 _____

_____

_____

3 _____

_____

What do you need to do in order to achieve your goals?

_____

_____

_____

Me time: what will you do for *you* this week?

April
2020

April 2020

Su	M	Tu	W	Th	F	Sa
			1	2	3	4
5	6	7	8	9	10	11
12	13	14	15	16	17	18
19	20	21	22	23	24	25
26	27	28	29	30		

MON 13	
TUE 14	
WED 15	
THUR 16	
FRI 17	
SAT 18	
SUN 19	

Checklist:

_____ ☐

_____ ☐

_____ ☐

_____ ☐

_____ ☐

_____ ☐

Notes:

_____

_____

_____

Reflections

What happened this week, and what did you learn?

A good plan will keep
you one step ahead.

Weekly Goal

List the top 3 goals you want to achieve this week:

1 _____
_____
_____

2 _____
_____
_____

3 _____
_____
_____

What do you need to do in order to achieve your goals?

_____
_____
_____

Me time: what will you do for *you* this week?

April
2020

April 2020
Su	M	Tu	W	Th	F	Sa
			1	2	3	4
5	6	7	8	9	10	11
12	13	14	15	16	17	18
19	20	21	22	23	24	25
26	27	28	29	30		

MON 20	
TUE 21	
WED 22	
THUR 23	
FRI 24	
SAT 25	
SUN 26	

Checklist:

_____ ☐

_____ ☐

_____ ☐

_____ ☐

_____ ☐

_____ ☐

Notes:

_____
_____
_____

Reflections

What happened this week, and what did you learn?

Communication is crucial.
Be clear and transparent.
Have a great week.

Weekly Goal

List the top 3 goals you want to achieve this week:

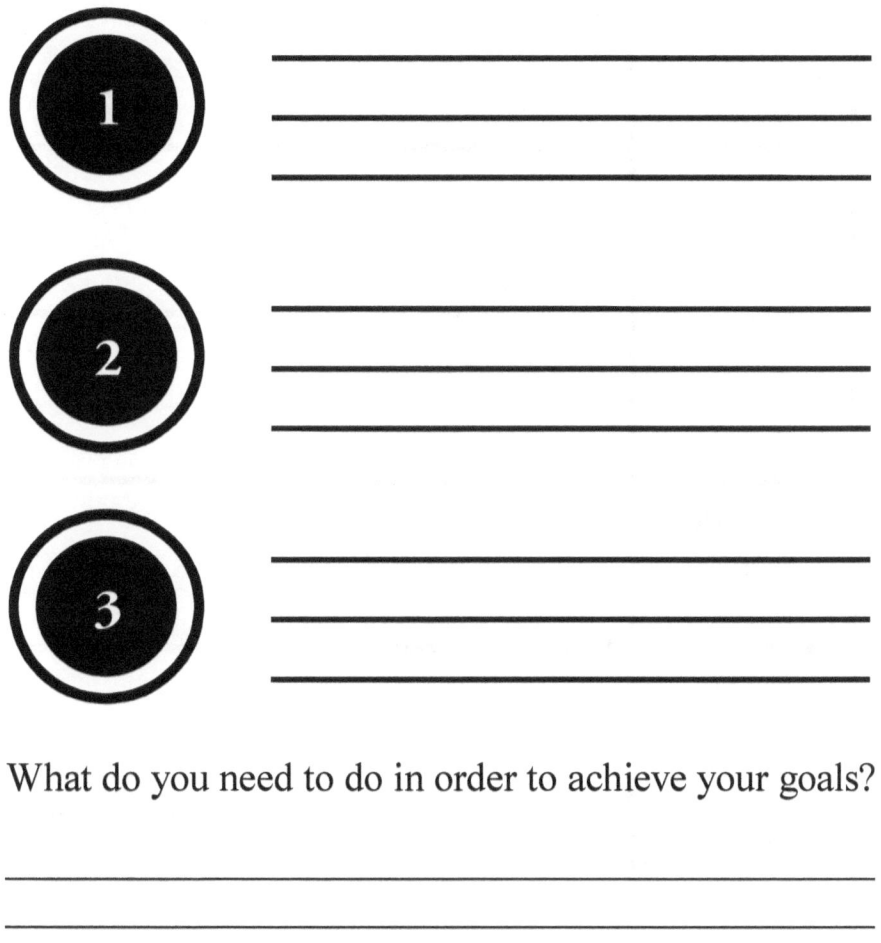

1 _____
_____
_____

2 _____
_____
_____

3 _____
_____
_____

What do you need to do in order to achieve your goals?

_____
_____
_____

Me time: what will you do for *you* this week?

April
2020

April 2020

Su	M	Tu	W	Th	F	Sa
			1	2	3	4
5	6	7	8	9	10	11
12	13	14	15	16	17	18
19	20	21	22	23	24	25
26	27	28	29	30		

MON 27	
TUE 28	
WED 29	
THUR 30	
FRI 01	
SAT 02	
SUN 03	

Checklist:

_____ ☐

_____ ☐

_____ ☐

_____ ☐

_____ ☐

_____ ☐

Notes:

_____

_____

_____

Reflections

What happened this week, and what did you learn?

You may not have all the answers, but challenge yourself to learn something new this week to update your knowledge.

Weekly Goal

List the top 3 goals you want to achieve this week:

What do you need to do in order to achieve your goals?

_____

_____

_____

Me time: what will you do for *you* this week?

May
2020

May 2020

Su	M	Tu	W	Th	F	Sa
					1	2
3	4	5	6	7	8	9
10	11	12	13	14	15	16
17	18	19	20	21	22	23
24	25	26	27	28	29	30
31						

MON 04	
TUE 05	
WED 06	
THUR 07	
FRI 08	
SAT 09	
SUN 10	

Checklist:

_____ ☐

_____ ☐

_____ ☐

_____ ☐

_____ ☐

_____ ☐

Notes:

_____

_____

_____

Reflections

What happened this week, and what did you learn?

You are enough and able
to succeed this week.

Weekly Goal

List the top 3 goals you want to achieve this week:

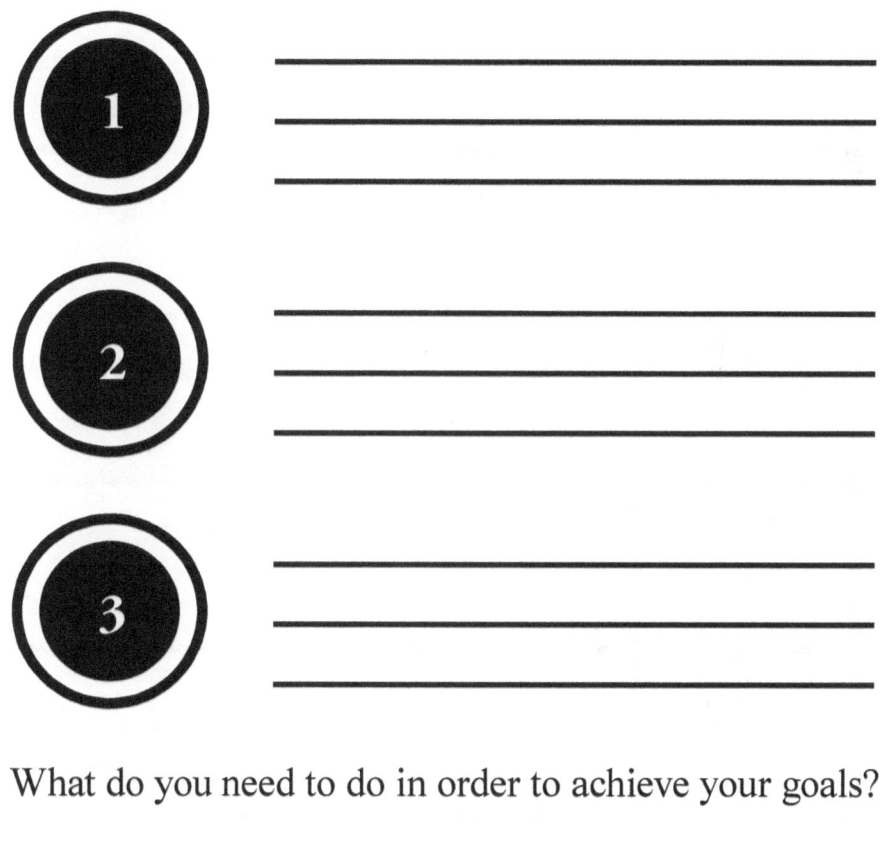

What do you need to do in order to achieve your goals?

_____

_____

_____

Me time: what will you do for *you* this week?

May
2020

May 2020

Su	M	Tu	W	Th	F	Sa
					1	2
3	4	5	6	7	8	9
10	11	12	13	14	15	16
17	18	19	20	21	22	23
24	25	26	27	28	29	30
31						

MON 11	
TUE 12	
WED 13	
THUR 14	
FRI 15	
SAT 16	
SUN 17	

Checklist:

_____ ☐

_____ ☐

_____ ☐

_____ ☐

_____ ☐

_____ ☐

Notes:

_____

_____

_____

Reflections

What happened this week, and what did you learn?

Mistakes happen.
Own them, and use them
to learn, develop, and
improve your practice.

Weekly Goal

List the top 3 goals you want to achieve this week:

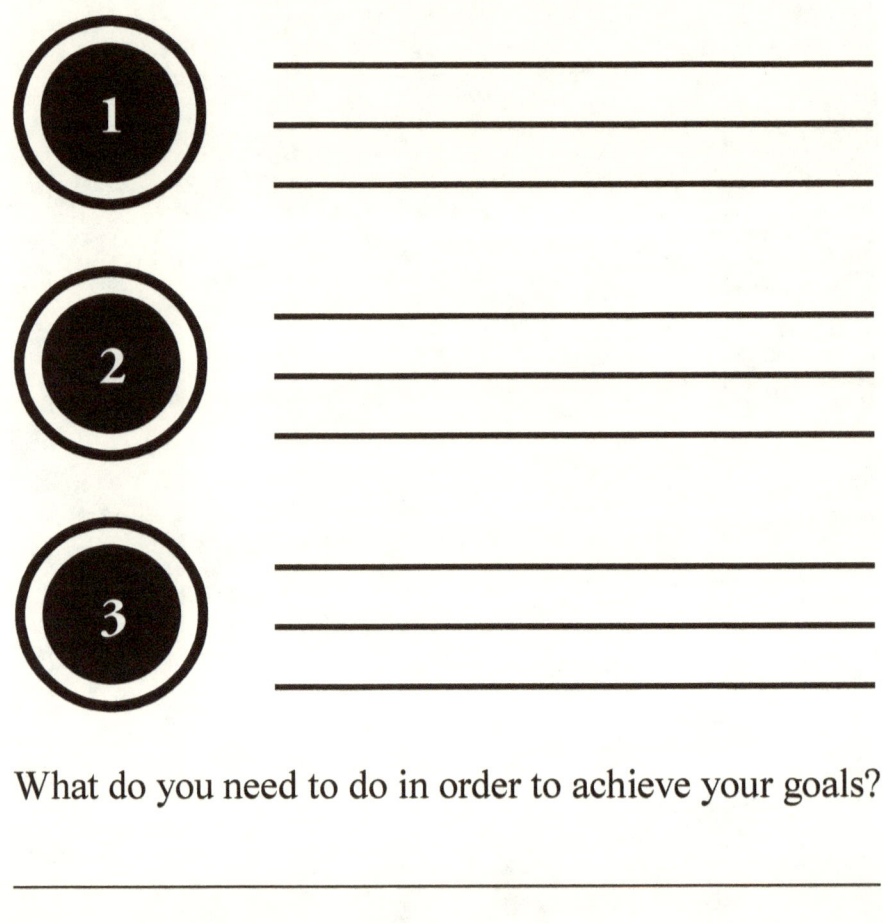

What do you need to do in order to achieve your goals?

_____
_____
_____

Me time: what will you do for *you* this week?

May
2020

May 2020

Su	M	Tu	W	Th	F	Sa
					1	2
3	4	5	6	7	8	9
10	11	12	13	14	15	16
17	18	19	20	21	22	23
24	25	26	27	28	29	30
31						

MON 18	
TUE 19	
WED 20	
THUR 21	
FRI 22	
SAT 23	
SUN 24	

Checklist:

☐

☐

☐

☐

☐

☐

Notes:

Reflections

What happened this week, and what did you learn?

When you improve your
practice, you ensure a good
experience for those you
provide a service to.

Weekly Goal

List the top 3 goals you want to achieve this week:

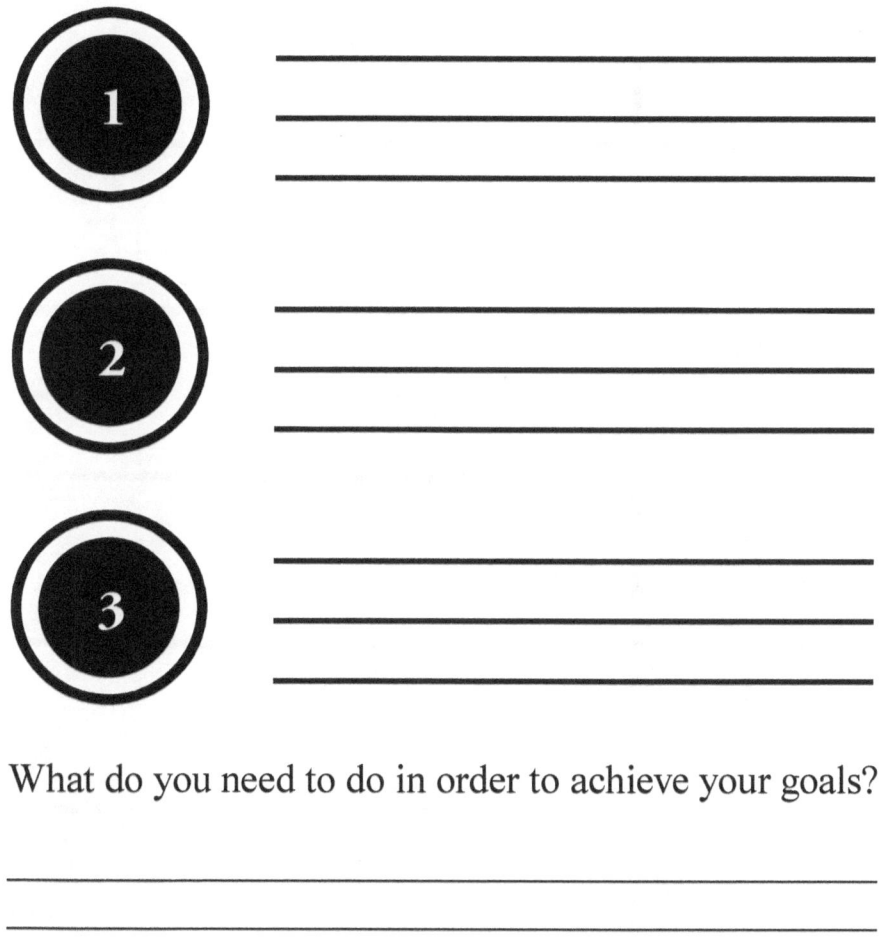

1 _____
_____
_____

2 _____
_____
_____

3 _____
_____
_____

What do you need to do in order to achieve your goals?

_____
_____
_____

Me time: what will you do for *you* this week?

May
2020

May 2020

Su	M	Tu	W	Th	F	Sa
					1	2
3	4	5	6	7	8	9
10	11	12	13	14	15	16
17	18	19	20	21	22	23
24	25	26	27	28	29	30
31						

MON 25	
TUE 26	
WED 27	
THUR 28	
FRI 29	
SAT 30	
SUN 31	

Checklist:

    ☐

_____

    ☐

_____

    ☐

_____

    ☐

_____

    ☐

_____

    ☐

_____

Notes:

_____
_____
_____

Reflections

What happened this week, and what did you learn?

Each day is a chance to start a new. What will you do differently this week?

Weekly Goal

List the top 3 goals you want to achieve this week:

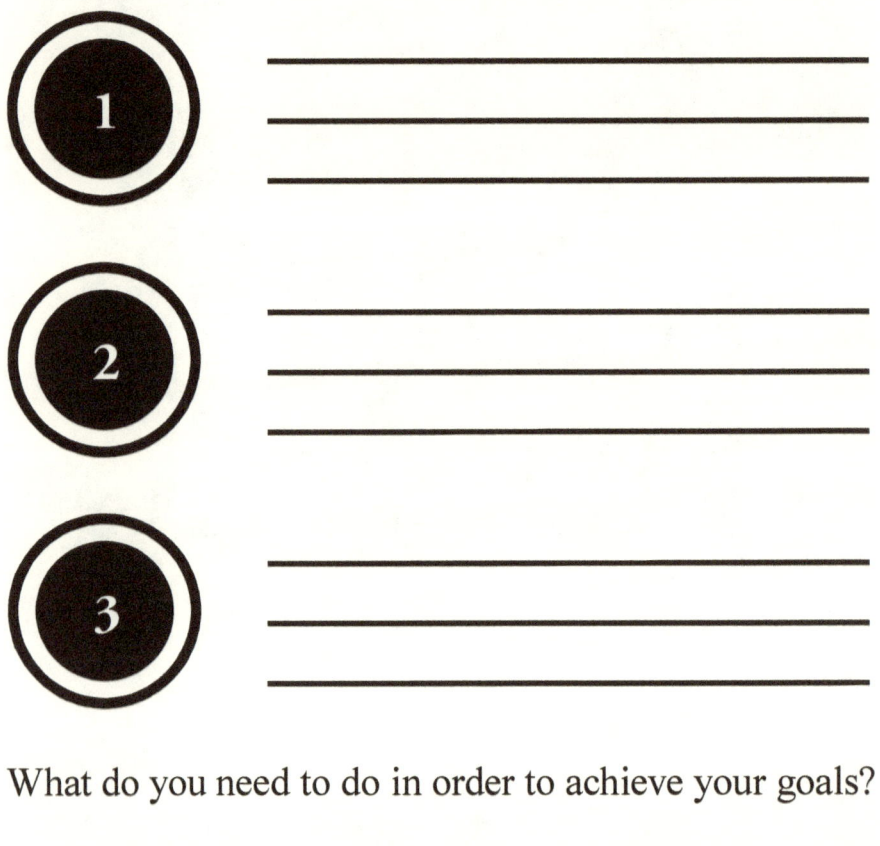

1 _____
_____
_____

2 _____
_____
_____

3 _____
_____
_____

What do you need to do in order to achieve your goals?

_____
_____
_____

Me time: what will you do for *you* this week?

June
2020

June 2020

Su	M	Tu	W	Th	F	Sa
	1	2	3	4	5	6
7	8	9	10	11	12	13
14	15	16	17	18	19	20
21	22	23	24	25	26	27
28	29	30				

MON 01	
TUE 02	
WED 03	
THUR 04	
FRI 05	
SAT 06	
SUN 07	

Checklist:

_____ ☐

_____ ☐

_____ ☐

_____ ☐

_____ ☐

_____ ☐

Notes:

_____

_____

_____

Reflections

What happened this week, and what did you learn?

A good plan goes
a long way.

Weekly Goal

List the top 3 goals you want to achieve this week:

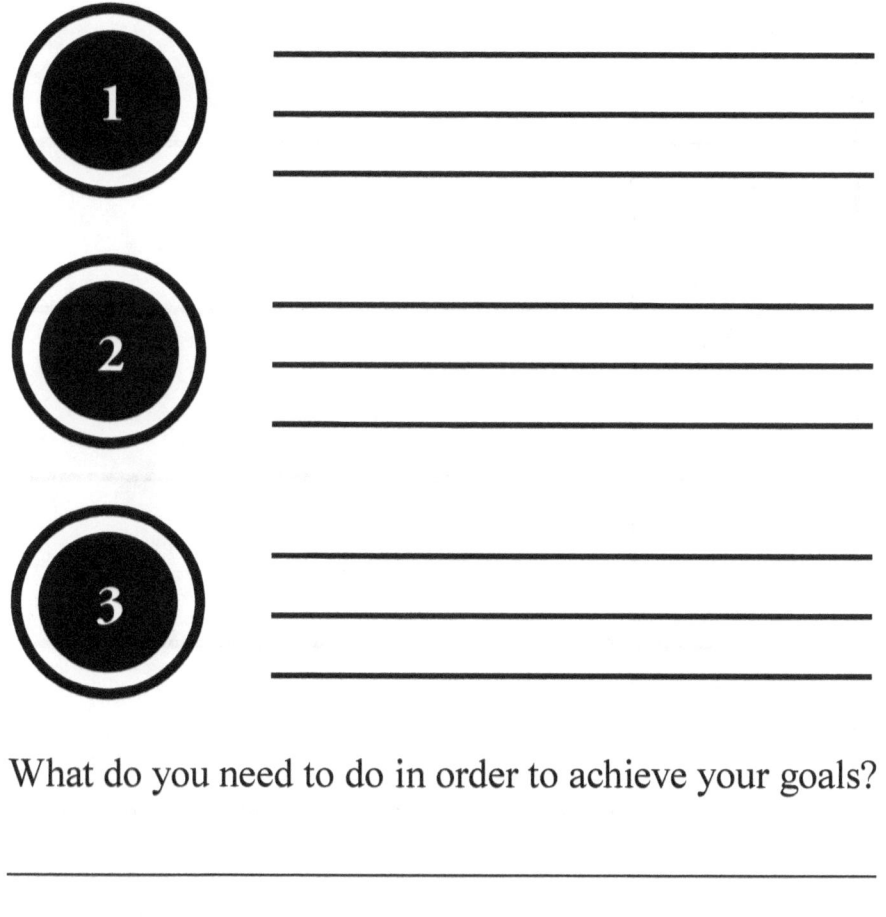

What do you need to do in order to achieve your goals?

_____

_____

_____

Me time: what will you do for *you* this week?

June
2020

June 2020

Su	M	Tu	W	Th	F	Sa
	1	2	3	4	5	6
7	8	9	10	11	12	13
14	15	16	17	18	19	20
21	22	23	24	25	26	27
28	29	30				

MON 08	
TUE 09	
WED 10	
THUR 11	
FRI 12	
SAT 13	
SUN 14	

Checklist:

☐

_____

☐

_____

☐

_____

☐

_____

☐

_____

☐

_____

Notes:

_____

_____

_____

Reflections

What happened this week, and what did you learn?

Your day can be filled with
unforeseen changes.
This means your plans
can always change.

Weekly Goal

List the top 3 goals you want to achieve this week:

1 _____
   _____
   _____

2 _____
   _____
   _____

3 _____
   _____
   _____

What do you need to do in order to achieve your goals?

_____
_____
_____

Me time: what will you do for *you* this week?

June
2020

June 2020						
Su	M	Tu	W	Th	F	Sa
	1	2	3	4	5	6
7	8	9	10	11	12	13
14	15	16	17	18	19	20
21	22	23	24	25	26	27
28	29	30				

MON 15	
TUE 16	
WED 17	
THUR 18	
FRI 19	
SAT 20	
SUN 21	

Checklist:

_____ ☐

_____ ☐

_____ ☐

_____ ☐

_____ ☐

_____ ☐

Notes:

_____

_____

_____

Reflections

What happened this week, and what did you learn?

Being flexible and
adaptable to change
makes all the difference.

Weekly Goal

List the top 3 goals you want to achieve this week:

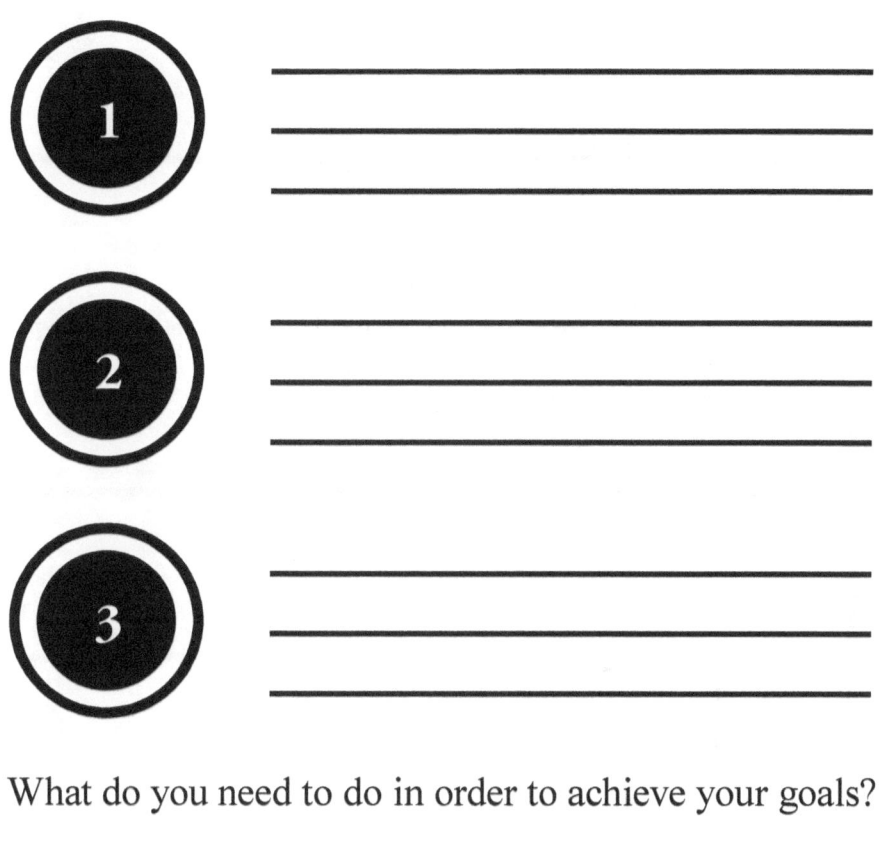

1 _____
_____
_____

2 _____
_____
_____

3 _____
_____

What do you need to do in order to achieve your goals?

_____
_____
_____

Me time: what will you do for *you* this week?

June
2020

June 2020

Su	M	Tu	W	Th	F	Sa
		1	2	3	4	5	6
7	8	9	10	11	12	13
14	15	16	17	18	19	20
21	22	23	24	25	26	27
28	29	30				

MON 22	
TUE 23	
WED 24	
THUR 25	
FRI 26	
SAT 27	
SUN 28	

Checklist:

_____ ☐

_____ ☐

_____ ☐

_____ ☐

_____ ☐

_____ ☐

Notes:

_____

_____

_____

Reflections

What happened this week, and what did you learn?

Learn to take care of
yourself first, before you
take care of others.
Don't forget to schedule
a rest day this week.

Weekly Goal

List the top 3 goals you want to achieve this week:

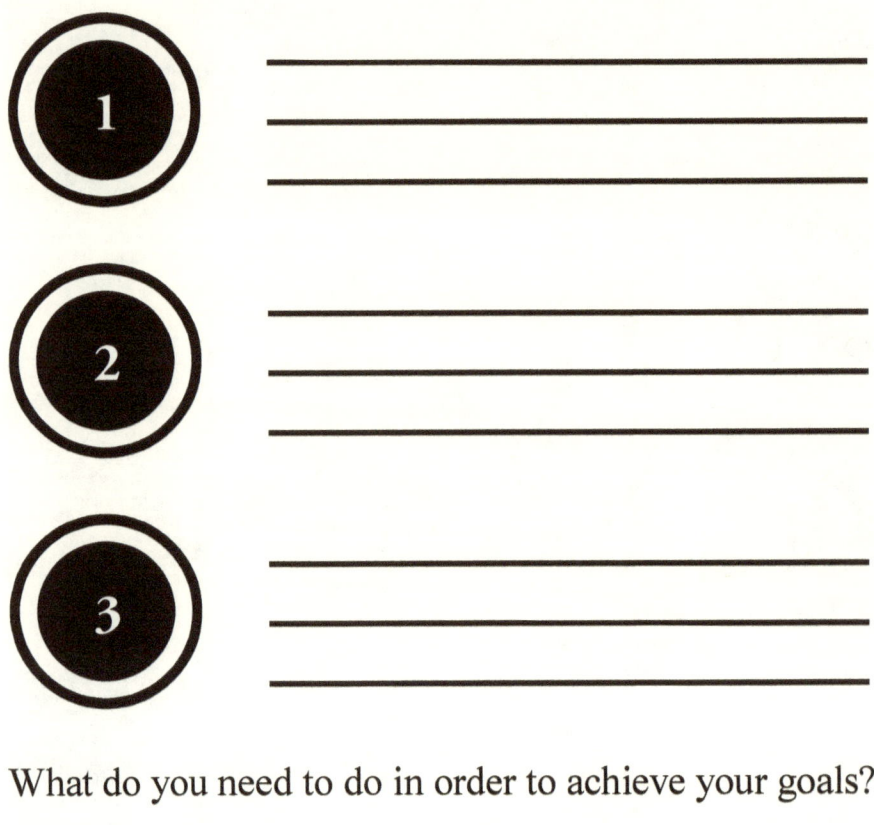

1 _____
_____
_____

2 _____
_____
_____

3 _____
_____
_____

What do you need to do in order to achieve your goals?

_____
_____
_____

> Me time: what will you do for *you* this week?

July
2020

July 2020
Su	M	Tu	W	Th	F	Sa
			1	2	3	4
5	6	7	8	9	10	11
12	13	14	15	16	17	18
19	20	21	22	23	24	25
26	27	28	29	30	31	

MON 29	
TUE 30	
WED 01	
THUR 02	
FRI 03	
SAT 04	
SUN 05	

Checklist:

_____ ☐

_____ ☐

_____ ☐

_____ ☐

_____ ☐

_____ ☐

Notes:

_____

_____

_____

Reflections

What happened this week, and what did you learn?

If nothing on your plan
was achieved last week,
have you utilised the
time effectively?

Weekly Goal

List the top 3 goals you want to achieve this week:

1 _____
_____
_____

2 _____
_____
_____

3 _____
_____
_____

What do you need to do in order to achieve your goals?

_____
_____
_____

Me time: what will you do for *you* this week?

July
2020

Su	M	Tu	W	Th	F	Sa
			1	2	3	4
5	6	7	8	9	10	11
12	13	14	15	16	17	18
19	20	21	22	23	24	25
26	27	28	29	30	31	

July 2020

MON 06	
TUE 07	
WED 08	
THUR 09	
FRI 10	
SAT 11	
SUN 12	

Checklist:

_____ ☐

_____ ☐

_____ ☐

_____ ☐

_____ ☐

_____ ☐

Notes:

_____

_____

_____

Reflections

What happened this week, and what did you learn?

Time goes so quickly,
but never overlook
your time to reflect
this week.

Weekly Goal

List the top 3 goals you want to achieve this week:

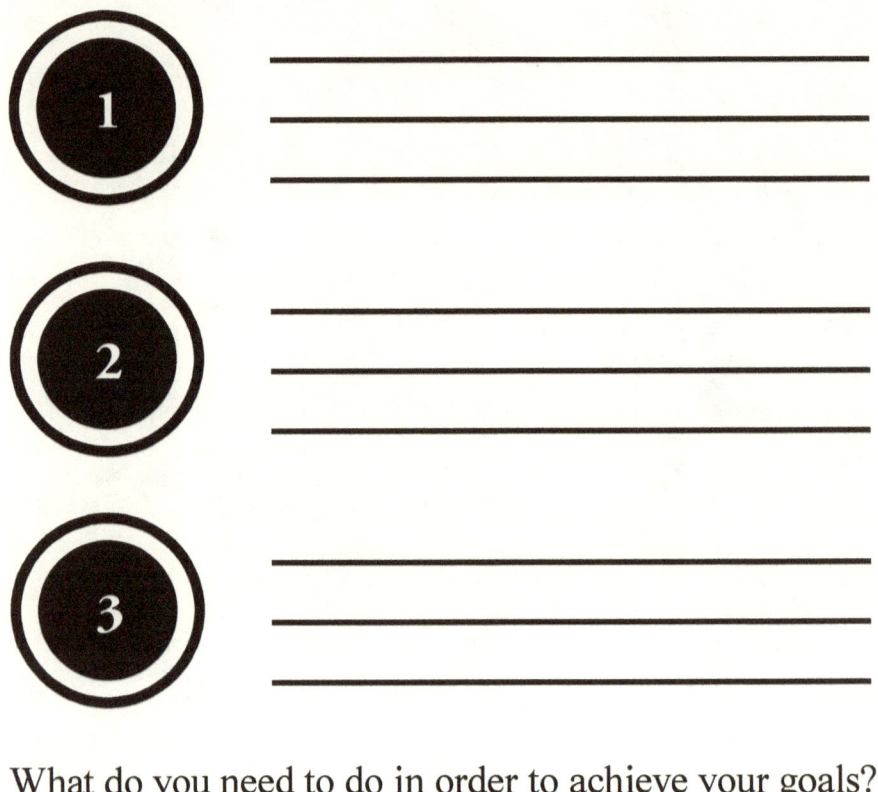

1 _____
_____
_____

2 _____
_____
_____

3 _____
_____
_____

What do you need to do in order to achieve your goals?

_____
_____
_____

Me time: what will you do for _you_ this week?

July
2020

July 2020						
Su	M	Tu	W	Th	F	Sa
			1	2	3	4
5	6	7	8	9	10	11
12	13	14	15	16	17	18
19	20	21	22	23	24	25
26	27	28	29	30	31	

MON 13	
TUE 14	
WED 15	
THUR 16	
FRI 17	
SAT 18	
SUN 19	

Checklist:

☐

☐

☐

☐

☐

☐

Notes:

Reflections

What happened this week, and what did you learn?

When there is so much
going on in your mind,
write a plan for your
own clarity.

Weekly Goal

List the top 3 goals you want to achieve this week:

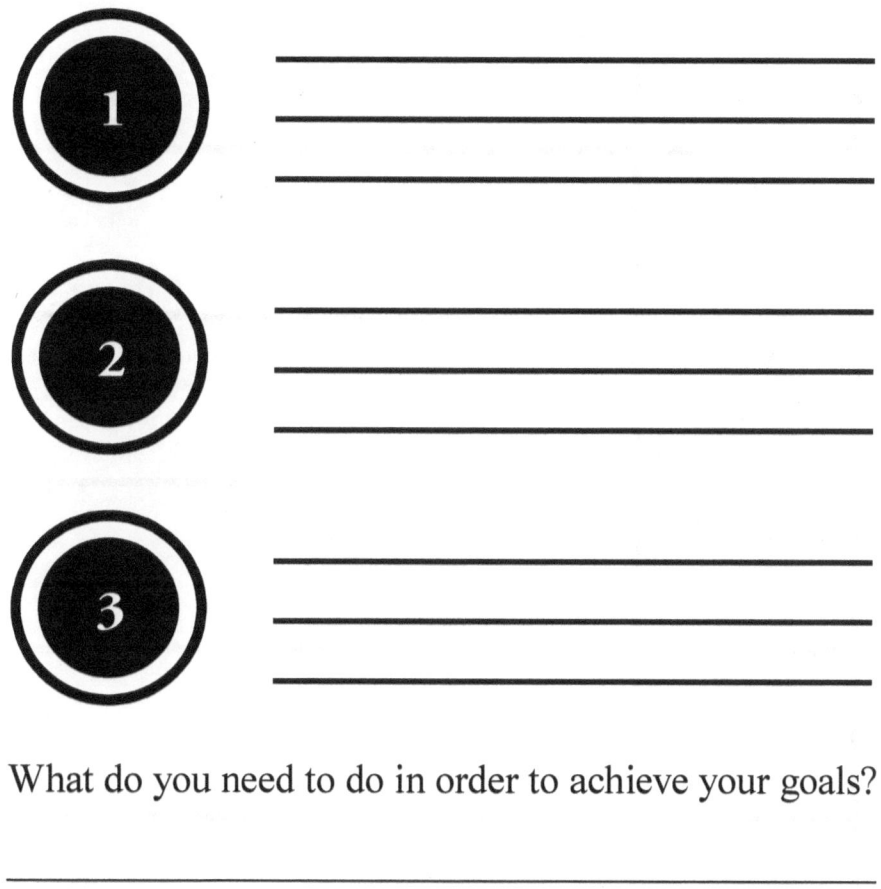

1

_____
_____
_____

2

_____
_____
_____

3

_____
_____
_____

What do you need to do in order to achieve your goals?

_____
_____
_____

Me time: what will you do for _you_ this week?

July
2020

July 2020						
Su	M	Tu	W	Th	F	Sa
			1	2	3	4
5	6	7	8	9	10	11
12	13	14	15	16	17	18
19	20	21	22	23	24	25
26	27	28	29	30	31	

MON 20	
TUE 21	
WED 22	
THUR 23	
FRI 24	
SAT 25	
SUN 26	

Checklist:

☐

☐

☐

☐

☐

☐

Notes:

Reflections

What happened this week, and what did you learn?

There is so much to
get done, but don't let that
take away from your
training days, which are
crucial for you to provide
better support to those
in need.

Weekly Goal

List the top 3 goals you want to achieve this week:

1 _____

2 _____

3 _____

What do you need to do in order to achieve your goals?

_____

_____

_____

Me time: what will you do for *you* this week?

July
2020

July 2020						
Su	M	Tu	W	Th	F	Sa
			1	2	3	4
5	6	7	8	9	10	11
12	13	14	15	16	17	18
19	20	21	22	23	24	25
26	27	28	29	30	31	

MON 27	
TUE 28	
WED 29	
THUR 30	
FRI 31	
SAT 01	
SUN 02	

Checklist:

_____ ☐

_____ ☐

_____ ☐

_____ ☐

_____ ☐

_____ ☐

Notes:

_____

_____

_____

Reflections

What happened this week, and what did you learn?

When things get overwhelming, take a deep breath, and then exhale. Go back to basics. You are in control of *you*.

Weekly Goal

List the top 3 goals you want to achieve this week:

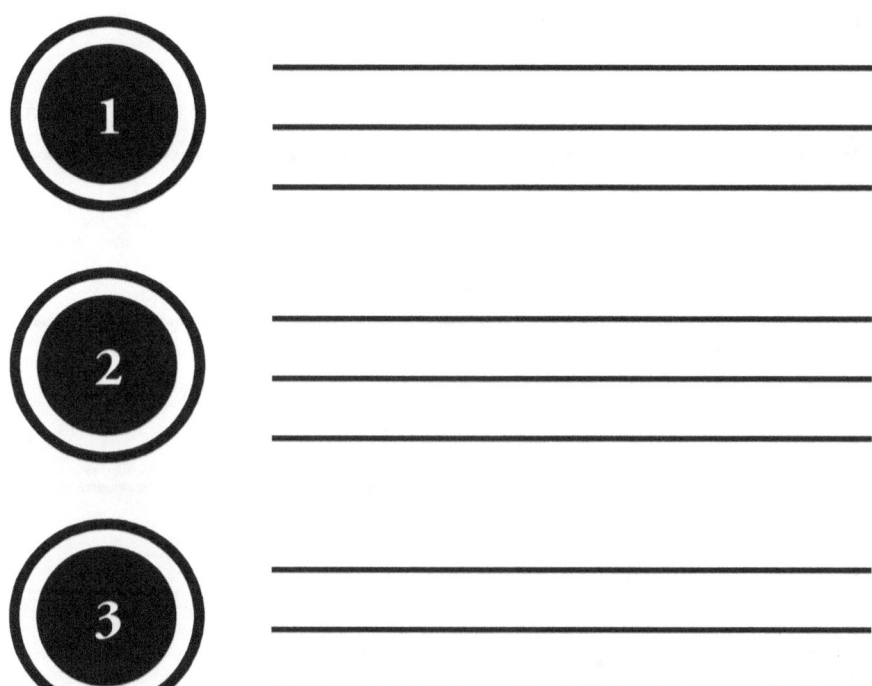

What do you need to do in order to achieve your goals?

_____

_____

_____

Me time: what will you do for *you* this week?

August
2020

August 2020

Su	M	Tu	W	Th	F	Sa
						1
2	3	4	5	6	7	8
9	10	11	12	13	14	15
16	17	18	19	20	21	22
23	24	25	26	27	28	29
30	31					

MON 03	
TUE 04	
WED 05	
THUR 06	
FRI 07	
SAT 08	
SUN 09	

Checklist:

_____ ☐

_____ ☐

_____ ☐

_____ ☐

_____ ☐

_____ ☐

Notes:

_____

_____

_____

Reflections

What happened this week, and what did you learn?

Smile, have an awesome
week, and achieve
your goals.

Weekly Goal

List the top 3 goals you want to achieve this week:

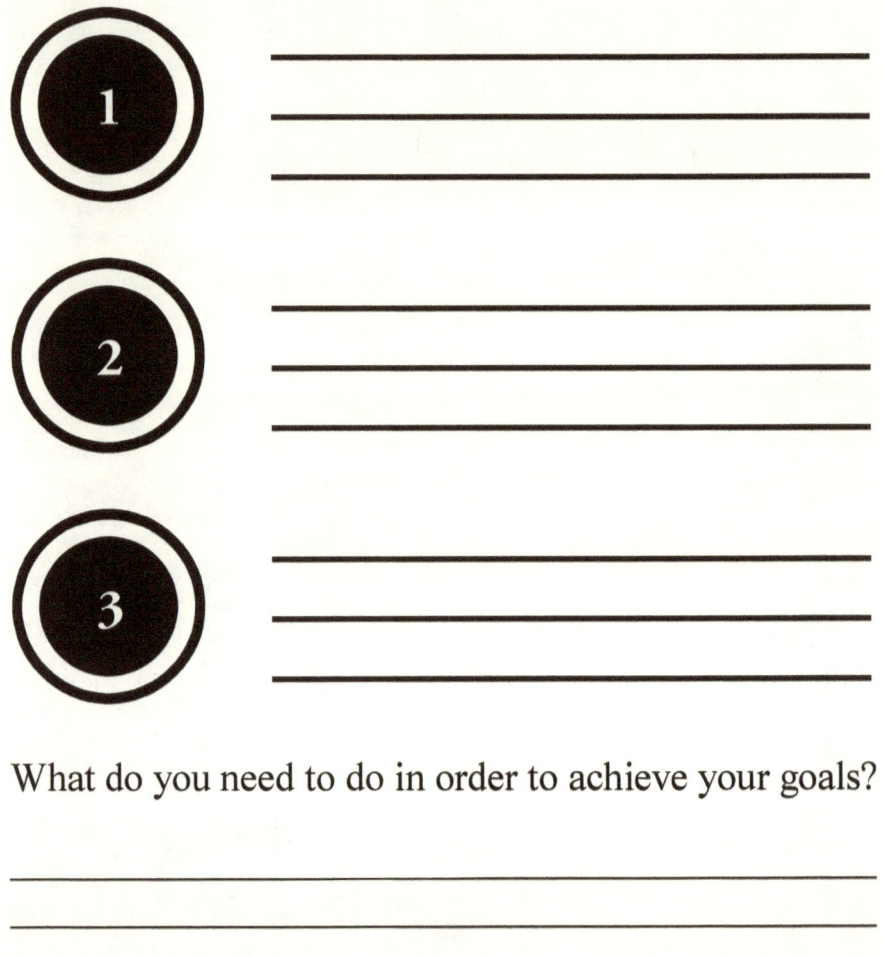

1 _____

_____

_____

2 _____

_____

_____

3 _____

_____

What do you need to do in order to achieve your goals?

_____

_____

_____

Me time: what will you do for *you* this week?

August
2020

August 2020

Su	M	Tu	W	Th	F	Sa
						1
2	3	4	5	6	7	8
9	10	11	12	13	14	15
16	17	18	19	20	21	22
23	24	25	26	27	28	29
30	31					

MON 10	
TUE 11	
WED 12	
THUR 13	
FRI 14	
SAT 15	
SUN 16	

Checklist:

_____ ☐

_____ ☐

_____ ☐

_____ ☐

_____ ☐

_____ ☐

Notes:

_____

_____

_____

Reflections

What happened this week, and what did you learn?

Keep going. You are
doing a great job.

Weekly Goal

List the top 3 goals you want to achieve this week:

1 _____
_____
_____

2 _____
_____
_____

3 _____
_____
_____

What do you need to do in order to achieve your goals?

_____
_____
_____

Me time: what will you do for *you* this week?

August
2020

August 2020

Su	M	Tu	W	Th	F	Sa
						1
2	3	4	5	6	7	8
9	10	11	12	13	14	15
16	17	18	19	20	21	22
23	24	25	26	27	28	29
30	31					

MON
17

TUE
18

WED
19

THUR
20

FRI
21

SAT
22

SUN
23

Checklist:

☐

☐

☐

☐

☐

☐

Notes:

Reflections

What happened this week, and what did you learn?

Better partnerships through networking can increase facilitation to the right information and services. Who will you connect with this week?

Weekly Goal

List the top 3 goals you want to achieve this week:

1

_____
_____
_____

2

_____
_____
_____

3

_____
_____
_____

What do you need to do in order to achieve your goals?

_____
_____
_____

Me time: what will you do for *you* this week?

August
2020

August 2020

Su	M	Tu	W	Th	F	Sa
						1
2	3	4	5	6	7	8
9	10	11	12	13	14	15
16	17	18	19	20	21	22
23	24	25	26	27	28	29
30	31					

MON 24	
TUE 25	
WED 26	
THUR 27	
FRI 28	
SAT 29	
SUN 30	

Checklist:

_____ ☐

_____ ☐

_____ ☐

_____ ☐

_____ ☐

_____ ☐

Notes:

_____

_____

_____

Reflections

What happened this week, and what did you learn?

Every day is a lesson to
help you grow and develop
your profession.

Weekly Goal

List the top 3 goals you want to achieve this week:

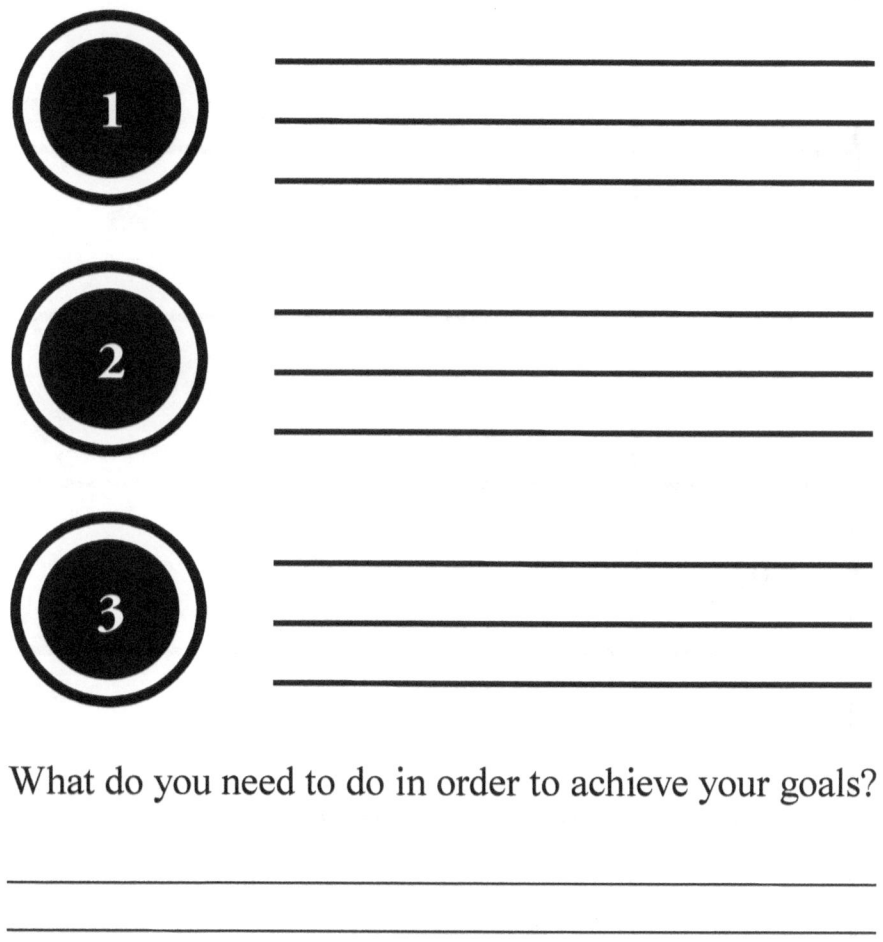

1

2

3

What do you need to do in order to achieve your goals?

Me time: what will you do for *you* this week?

September
2020

September 2020

Su	M	Tu	W	Th	F	Sa
		1	2	3	4	5
6	7	8	9	10	11	12
13	14	15	16	17	18	19
20	21	22	23	24	25	26
27	28	29	30			

MON 31	
TUE 01	
WED 02	
THUR 03	
FRI 04	
SAT 05	
SUN 06	

Checklist:

_____ ☐

_____ ☐

_____ ☐

_____ ☐

_____ ☐

_____ ☐

Notes:

_____

_____

_____

Reflections

What happened this week, and what did you learn?

You can only do your best
with the resources
available to you.

Weekly Goal

List the top 3 goals you want to achieve this week:

1. _____
   _____
   _____

2. _____
   _____
   _____

3. _____
   _____
   _____

What do you need to do in order to achieve your goals?

_____
_____
_____

Me time: what will you do for *you* this week?

September
2020

September 2020

Su	M	Tu	W	Th	F	Sa
		1	2	3	4	5
6	7	8	9	10	11	12
13	14	15	16	17	18	19
20	21	22	23	24	25	26
27	28	29	30			

MON 07	
TUE 08	
WED 09	
THUR 10	
FRI 11	
SAT 12	
SUN 13	

Checklist:

_____ ☐

_____ ☐

_____ ☐

_____ ☐

_____ ☐

_____ ☐

Notes:

_____

_____

_____

Reflections

What happened this week, and what did you learn?

The working week can take a lot of energy. It is important to build back that energy before the next week begins.

Weekly Goal

List the top 3 goals you want to achieve this week:

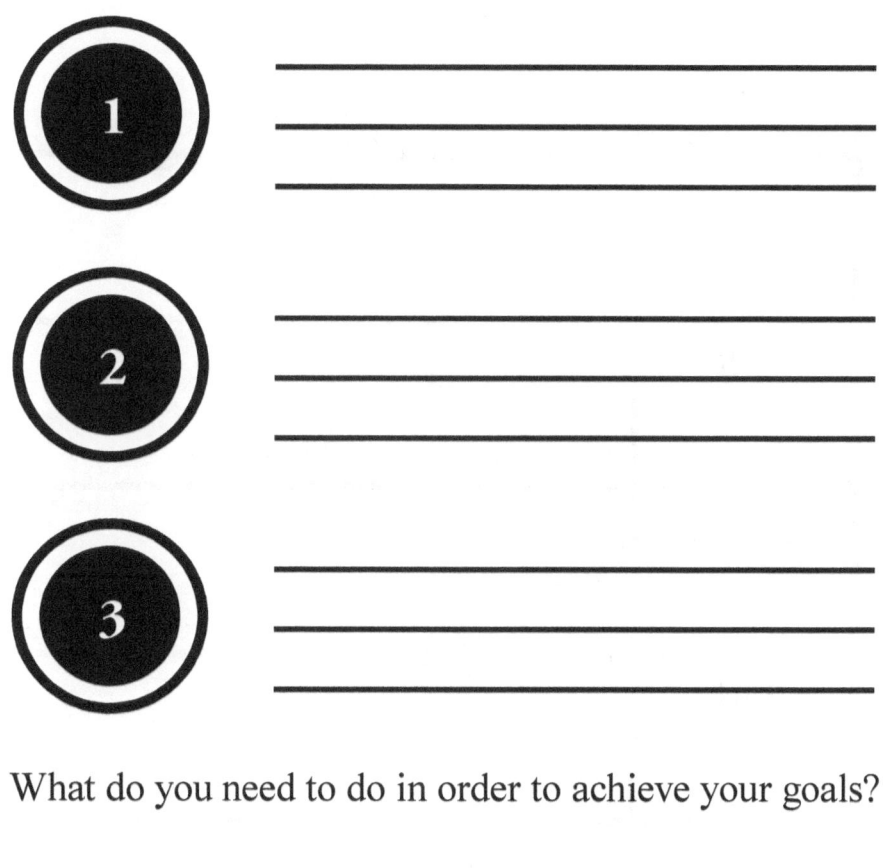

1 _____
_____
_____

2 _____
_____
_____

3 _____
_____
_____

What do you need to do in order to achieve your goals?

_____
_____
_____

Me time: what will you do for *you* this week?

September
2020

September 2020

Su	M	Tu	W	Th	F	Sa
		1	2	3	4	5
6	7	8	9	10	11	12
13	14	15	16	17	18	19
20	21	22	23	24	25	26
27	28	29	30			

MON 14	
TUE 15	
WED 16	
THUR 17	
FRI 18	
SAT 19	
SUN 20	

Checklist:

_____ ☐

_____ ☐

_____ ☐

_____ ☐

_____ ☐

_____ ☐

Notes:

_____

_____

_____

Reflections

What happened this week, and what did you learn?

Are you able to shut off
from your day when you
get home? If not, think
about what you can do
to achieve this and
implement itthis week.

Weekly Goal

List the top 3 goals you want to achieve this week:

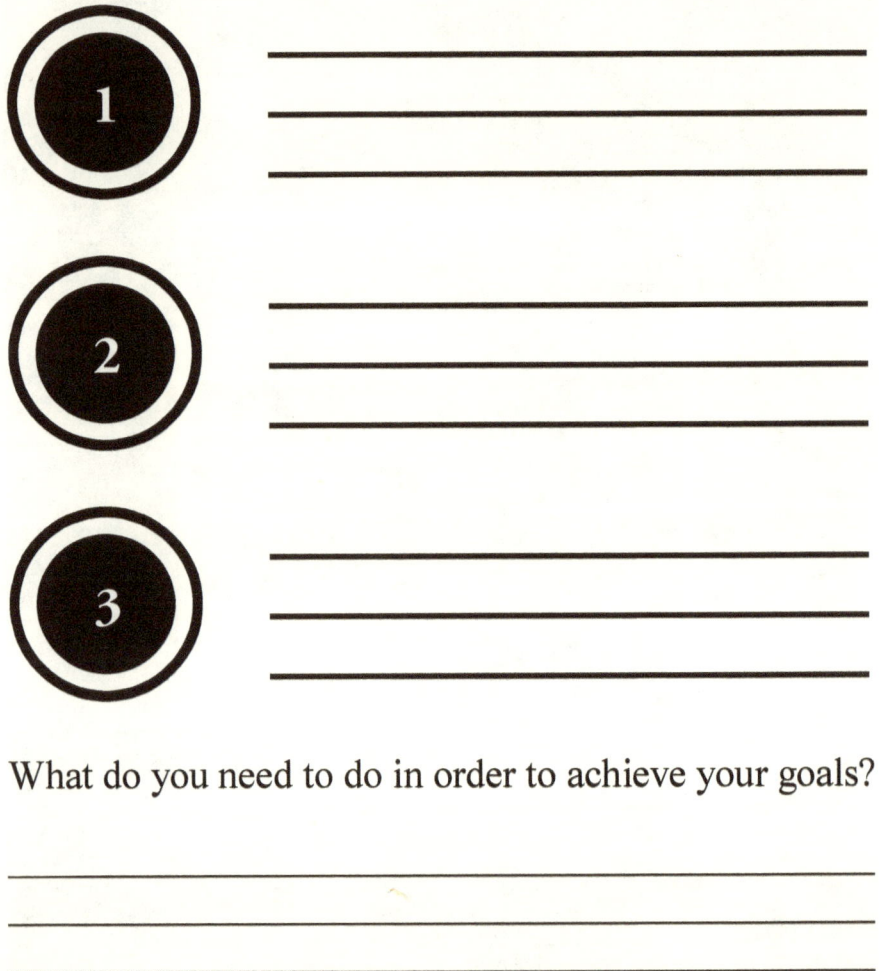

1 _____
_____
_____

2 _____
_____
_____

3 _____
_____
_____

What do you need to do in order to achieve your goals?

_____
_____
_____

Me time: what will you do for *you* this week?

September
2020

September 2020

Su	M	Tu	W	Th	F	Sa
		1	2	3	4	5
6	7	8	9	10	11	12
13	14	15	16	17	18	19
20	21	22	23	24	25	26
27	28	29	30			

MON 21	
TUE 22	
WED 23	
THUR 24	
FRI 25	
SAT 26	
SUN 27	

Checklist:

_____ ☐

_____ ☐

_____ ☐

_____ ☐

_____ ☐

_____ ☐

Notes:

_____

_____

_____

Reflections

What happened this week, and what did you learn?

Time matters, and how
you use it counts.

Weekly Goal

List the top 3 goals you want to achieve this week:

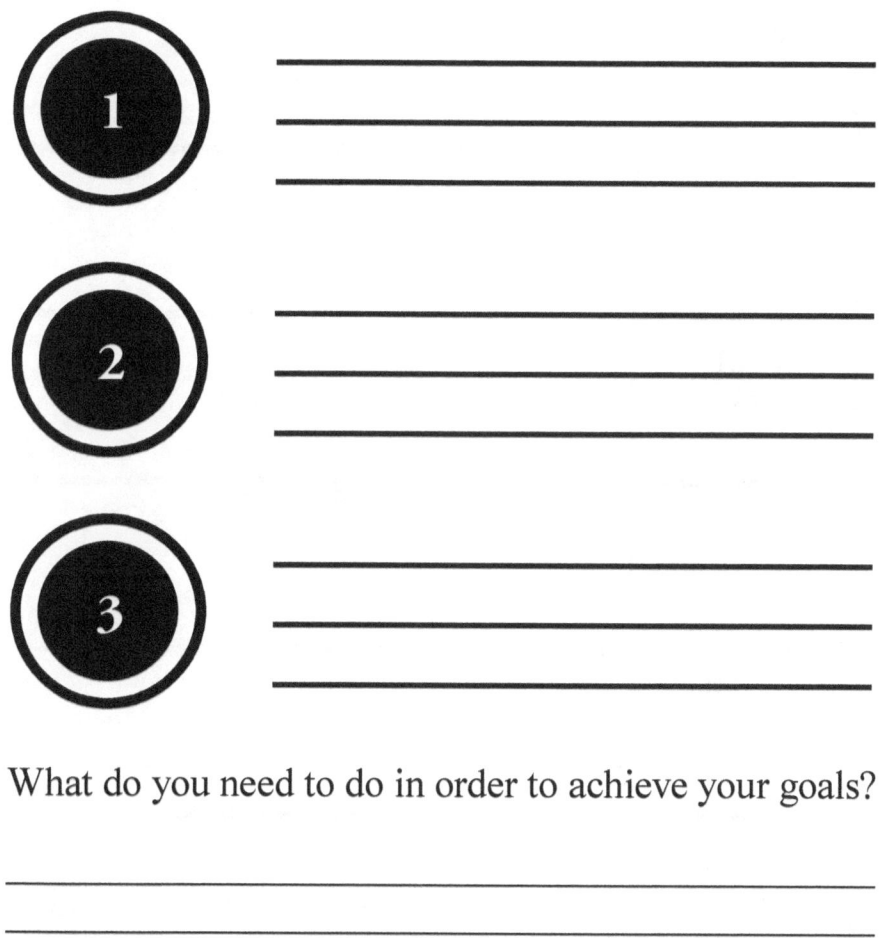

1 _____
_____
_____

2 _____
_____
_____

3 _____
_____
_____

What do you need to do in order to achieve your goals?

_____
_____
_____

Me time: what will you do for *you* this week?

October
2020

October 2020

Su	M	Tu	W	Th	F	Sa
				1	2	3
4	5	6	7	8	9	10
11	12	13	14	15	16	17
18	19	20	21	22	23	24
25	26	27	28	29	30	31

MON 28	
TUE 29	
WED 30	
THUR 01	
FRI 02	
SAT 03	
SUN 04	

Checklist:

_____ ☐

_____ ☐

_____ ☐

_____ ☐

_____ ☐

_____ ☐

Notes:

_____
_____
_____

Reflections

What happened this week, and what did you learn?

Setting boundaries on
how you utilise your time
where possible protects
you and those to whom
you provide a service.

Weekly Goal

List the top 3 goals you want to achieve this week:

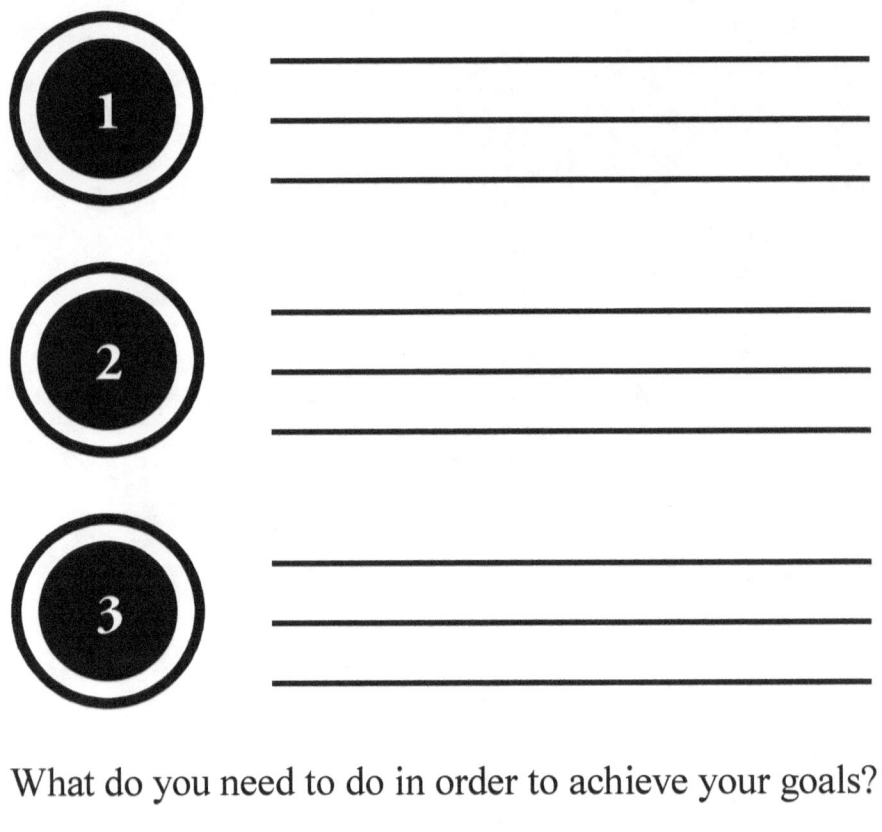

1 _____
_____
_____

2 _____
_____
_____

3 _____
_____
_____

What do you need to do in order to achieve your goals?

_____
_____
_____

Me time: what will you do for *you* this week?

October
2020

October 2020

Su	M	Tu	W	Th	F	Sa
				1	2	3
4	5	6	7	8	9	10
11	12	13	14	15	16	17
18	19	20	21	22	23	24
25	26	27	28	29	30	31

MON 05	
TUE 06	
WED 07	
THUR 08	
FRI 09	
SAT 10	
SUN 11	

Checklist:

☐

_____

☐

_____

☐

_____

☐

_____

☐

_____

☐

Notes:

_____
_____
_____

Reflections

What happened this week, and what did you learn?

Do not skip your lunch
breaks this week.
Take care of *you*.

Weekly Goal

List the top 3 goals you want to achieve this week:

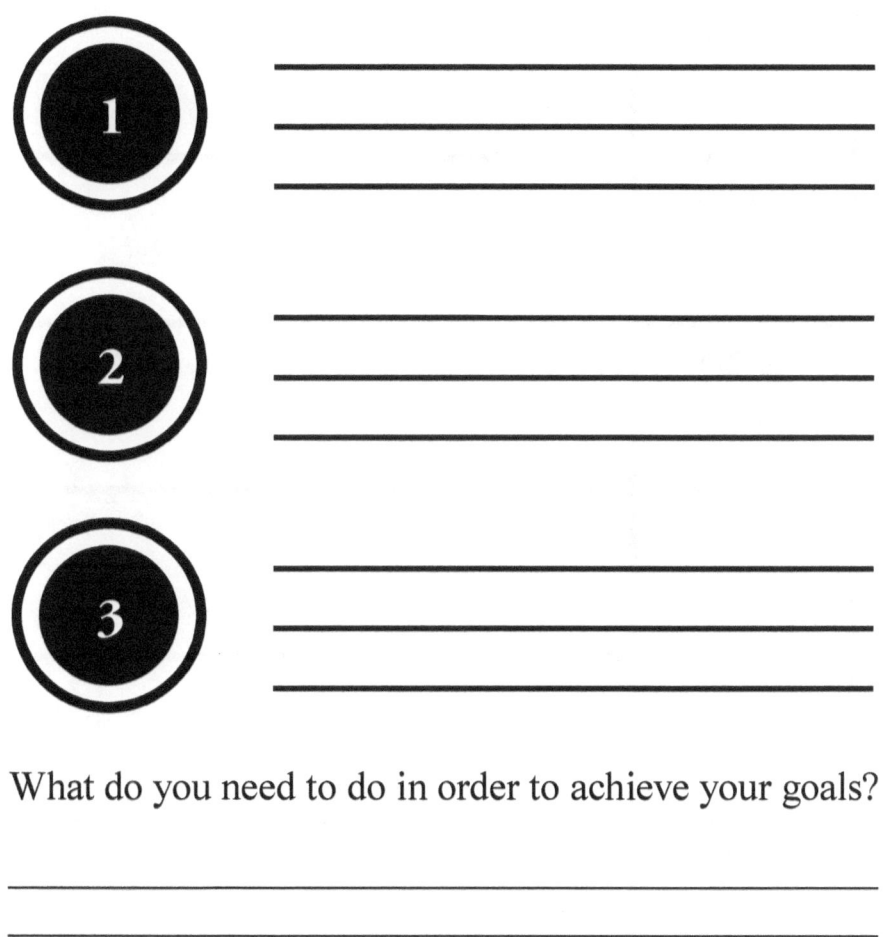

1 _____
_____
_____

2 _____
_____
_____

3 _____
_____

What do you need to do in order to achieve your goals?

_____
_____
_____

Me time: what will you do for *you* this week?

October
2020

October 2020

Su	M	Tu	W	Th	F	Sa
				1	2	3
4	5	6	7	8	9	10
11	12	13	14	15	16	17
18	19	20	21	22	23	24
25	26	27	28	29	30	31

MON 12	
TUE 13	
WED 14	
THUR 15	
FRI 16	
SAT 17	
SUN 18	

Checklist:

_____ ☐

_____ ☐

_____ ☐

_____ ☐

_____ ☐

_____ ☐

Notes:

_____

_____

_____

Reflections

What happened this week, and what did you learn?

This week is going to
be a good week.

Weekly Goal

List the top 3 goals you want to achieve this week:

1 _____
_____
_____

2 _____
_____
_____

3 _____
_____
_____

What do you need to do in order to achieve your goals?

_____
_____
_____

Me time: what will you do for *you* this week?

October
2020

October 2020

Su	M	Tu	W	Th	F	Sa
				1	2	3
4	5	6	7	8	9	10
11	12	13	14	15	16	17
18	19	20	21	22	23	24
25	26	27	28	29	30	31

MON
19

TUE
20

WED
21

THUR
22

FRI
23

SAT
24

SUN
25

Checklist:

_____ ☐

_____ ☐

_____ ☐

_____ ☐

_____ ☐

_____ ☐

Notes:

_____

_____

_____

Reflections

What happened this week, and what did you learn?

If last week did not go
according to plan,
that's OK.
Try again this week.

Weekly Goal

List the top 3 goals you want to achieve this week:

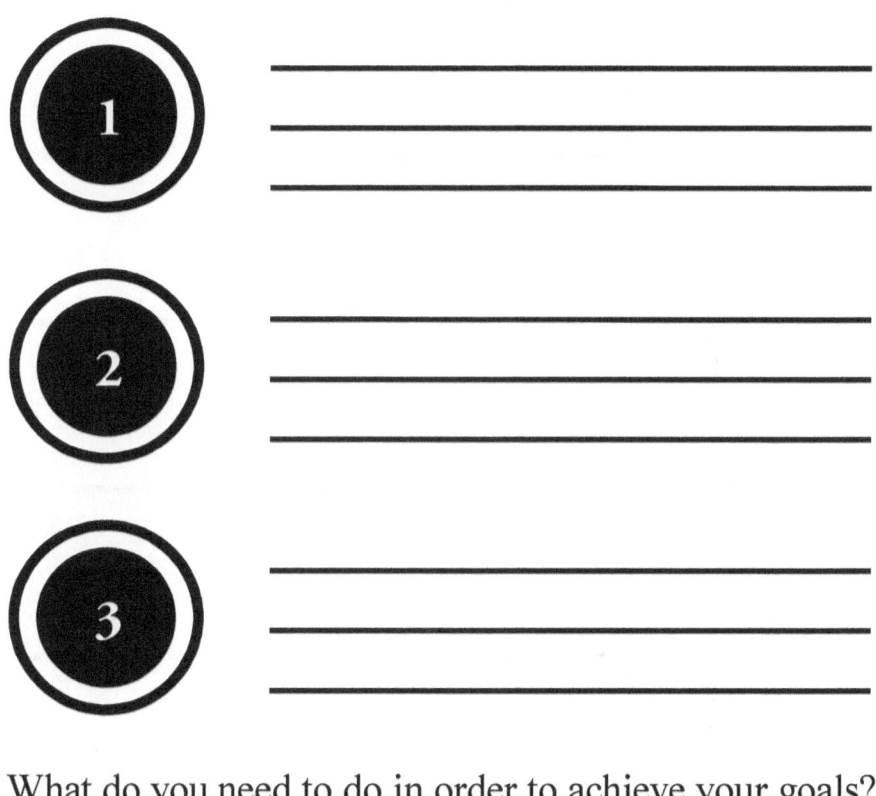

1 _____
_____
_____

2 _____
_____
_____

3 _____
_____

What do you need to do in order to achieve your goals?

_____
_____
_____

Me time: what will you do for *you* this week?

October
2020

October 2020

Su	M	Tu	W	Th	F	Sa
				1	2	3
4	5	6	7	8	9	10
11	12	13	14	15	16	17
18	19	20	21	22	23	24
25	26	27	28	29	30	31

MON 26	
TUE 27	
WED 28	
THUR 29	
FRI 30	
SAT 31	
SUN 01	

Checklist:

_____ ☐

_____ ☐

_____ ☐

_____ ☐

_____ ☐

_____ ☐

Notes:

_____

_____

_____

Reflections

What happened this week, and what did you learn?

You can achieve the goals
you have set for yourself
this week.

Weekly Goal

List the top 3 goals you want to achieve this week:

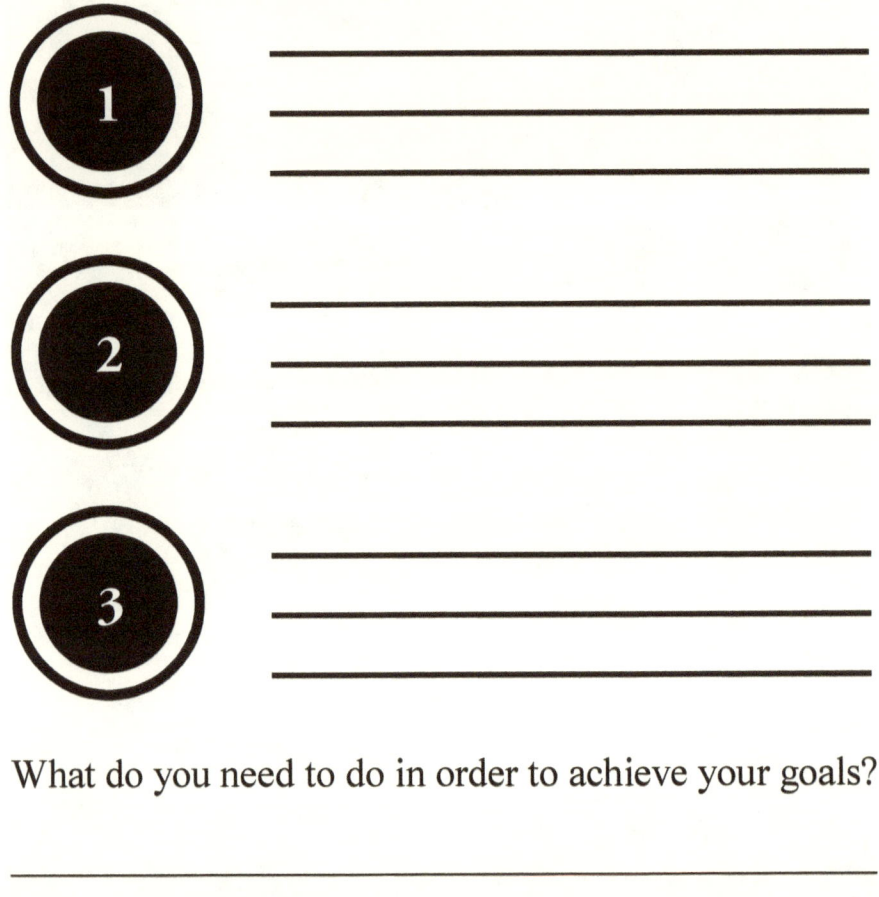

1 _____
_____
_____

2 _____
_____
_____

3 _____
_____
_____

What do you need to do in order to achieve your goals?

_____
_____
_____

Me time: what will you do for *you* this week?

November
2020

November 2020

Su	M	Tu	W	Th	F	Sa
1	2	3	4	5	6	7
8	9	10	11	12	13	14
15	16	17	18	19	20	21
22	23	24	25	26	27	28
29	30					

MON 02	
TUE 03	
WED 04	
THUR 05	
FRI 06	
SAT 07	
SUN 08	

Checklist:

_____ ☐

_____ ☐

_____ ☐

_____ ☐

_____ ☐

_____ ☐

Notes:

_____

_____

_____

Reflections

What happened this week, and what did you learn?

Consistency in your planning will help to achieve work/life balance.

Weekly Goal

List the top 3 goals you want to achieve this week:

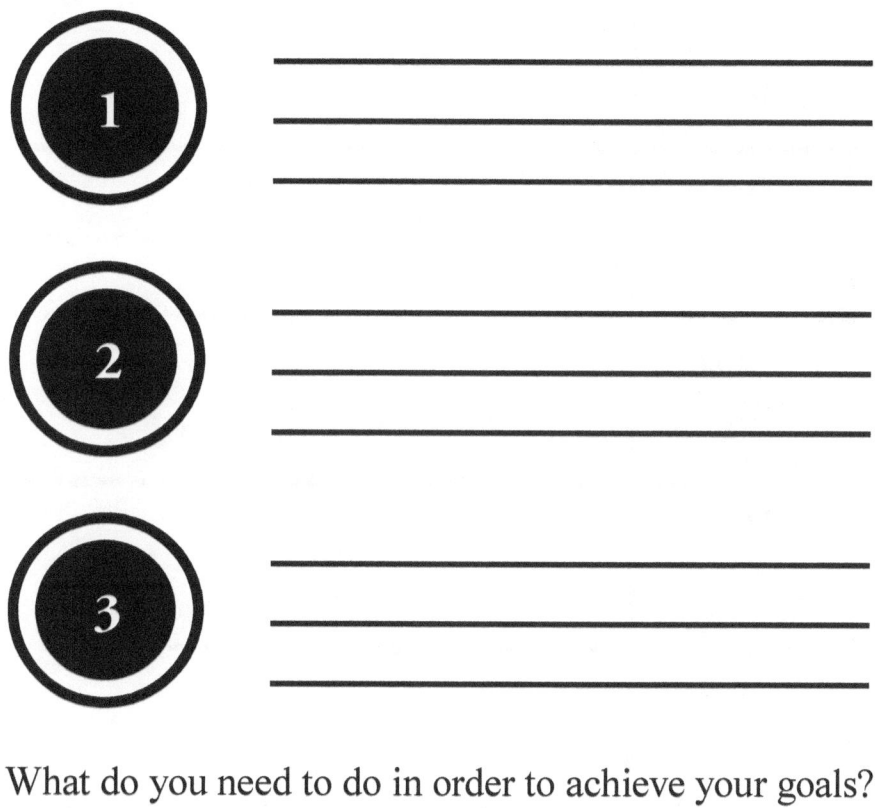

1 _____
_____
_____

2 _____
_____
_____

3 _____
_____

What do you need to do in order to achieve your goals?

_____
_____
_____

Me time: what will you do for *you* this week?

November
2020

November 2020

Su	M	Tu	W	Th	F	Sa
1	2	3	4	5	6	7
8	9	10	11	12	13	14
15	16	17	18	19	20	21
22	23	24	25	26	27	28
29	30					

MON 09	
TUE 10	
WED 11	
THUR 12	
FRI 13	
SAT 14	
SUN 15	

Checklist:

_____ ☐

_____ ☐

_____ ☐

_____ ☐

_____ ☐

_____ ☐

Notes:

_____

_____

_____

Reflections

What happened this week, and what did you learn?

Using your checklist as
well as weekly reflection
will help you to structure
your thoughts and
clear your mind.

Weekly Goal

List the top 3 goals you want to achieve this week:

1 _____
_____
_____

2 _____
_____
_____

3 _____
_____
_____

What do you need to do in order to achieve your goals?

_____
_____
_____

Me time: what will you do for *you* this week?

November
2020

November 2020

Su	M	Tu	W	Th	F	Sa
1	2	3	4	5	6	7
8	9	10	11	12	13	14
15	16	17	18	19	20	21
22	23	24	25	26	27	28
29	30					

MON 16	
TUE 17	
WED 18	
THUR 19	
FRI 20	
SAT 21	
SUN 22	

Checklist:

☐

_____

☐

_____

☐

_____

☐

_____

☐

_____

☐

_____

Notes:

_____

_____

_____

Reflections

What happened this week, and what did you learn?

You are stronger
than you think.

Weekly Goal

List the top 3 goals you want to achieve this week:

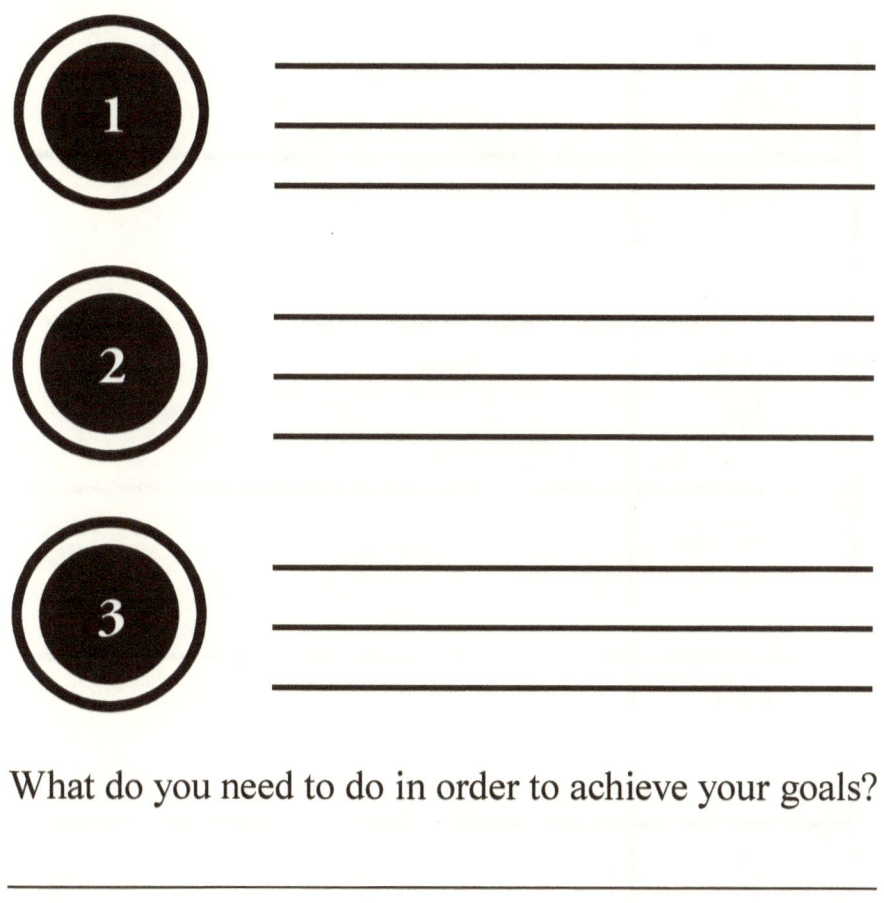

1

2

3

What do you need to do in order to achieve your goals?

Me time: what will you do for *you* this week?

November
2020

November 2020

Su	M	Tu	W	Th	F	Sa
1	2	3	4	5	6	7
8	9	10	11	12	13	14
15	16	17	18	19	20	21
22	23	24	25	26	27	28
29	30					

MON 23	
TUE 24	
WED 25	
THUR 26	
FRI 27	
SAT 28	
SUN 29	

Checklist:

_____ ☐

_____ ☐

_____ ☐

_____ ☐

_____ ☐

_____ ☐

Notes:

_____

_____

_____

Reflections

What happened this week, and what did you learn?

How do you do your job
week after week?
Emotional resilience
is key.

Weekly Goal

List the top 3 goals you want to achieve this week:

What do you need to do in order to achieve your goals?

_____

_____

_____

Me time: what will you do for *you* this week?

December
2020

December 2020

Su	M	Tu	W	Th	F	Sa
		1	2	3	4	5
6	7	8	9	10	11	12
13	14	15	16	17	18	19
20	21	22	23	24	25	26
27	28	29	30	31		

MON 30	
TUE 01	
WED 02	
THUR 03	
FRI 04	
SAT 05	
SUN 06	

Checklist:

_____ ☐

_____ ☐

_____ ☐

_____ ☐

_____ ☐

_____ ☐

Notes:

_____

_____

_____

Reflections

What happened this week, and what did you learn?

Sometimes there is so much to do that it can be overwhelming to know where to start.
Start with a plan.

Weekly Goal

List the top 3 goals you want to achieve this week:

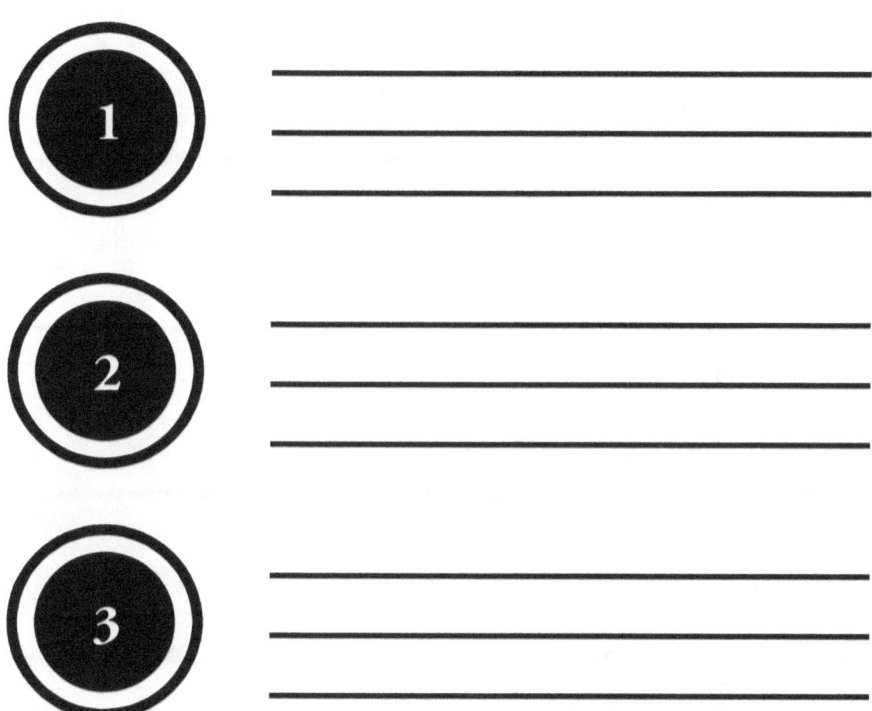

1 _____
_____
_____

2 _____
_____
_____

3 _____
_____
_____

What do you need to do in order to achieve your goals?

_____
_____
_____

Me time: what will you do for *you* this week?

December
2020

December 2020
Su	M	Tu	W	Th	F	Sa
		1	2	3	4	5
6	7	8	9	10	11	12
13	14	15	16	17	18	19
20	21	22	23	24	25	26
27	28	29	30	31		

MON 07	
TUE 08	
WED 09	
THUR 10	
FRI 11	
SAT 12	
SUN 13	

Checklist:

_____ ☐

_____ ☐

_____ ☐

_____ ☐

_____ ☐

_____ ☐

Notes:

_____

_____

_____

Reflections

What happened this week, and what did you learn?

Thank you for what you
do day after day and
week after week.

Weekly Goal

List the top 3 goals you want to achieve this week:

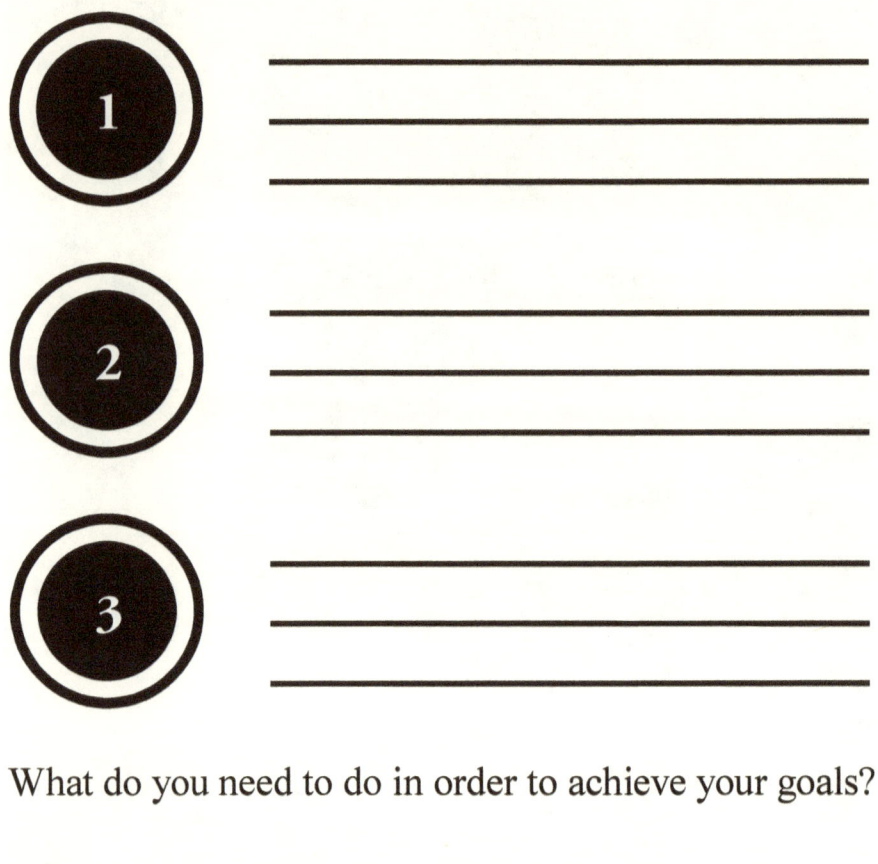

1 _____
_____
_____

2 _____
_____
_____

3 _____
_____
_____

What do you need to do in order to achieve your goals?

_____
_____
_____

Me time: what will you do for *you* this week?

December
2020

December 2020

Su	M	Tu	W	Th	F	Sa
		1	2	3	4	5
6	7	8	9	10	11	12
13	14	15	16	17	18	19
20	21	22	23	24	25	26
27	28	29	30	31		

MON 14	
TUE 15	
WED 16	
THUR 17	
FRI 18	
SAT 19	
SUN 20	

Checklist:

_____ ☐

_____ ☐

_____ ☐

_____ ☐

_____ ☐

_____ ☐

Notes:

_____

_____

_____

Reflections

What happened this week, and what did you learn?

It's never too late to plan.
Have a great week.

Weekly Goal

List the top 3 goals you want to achieve this week:

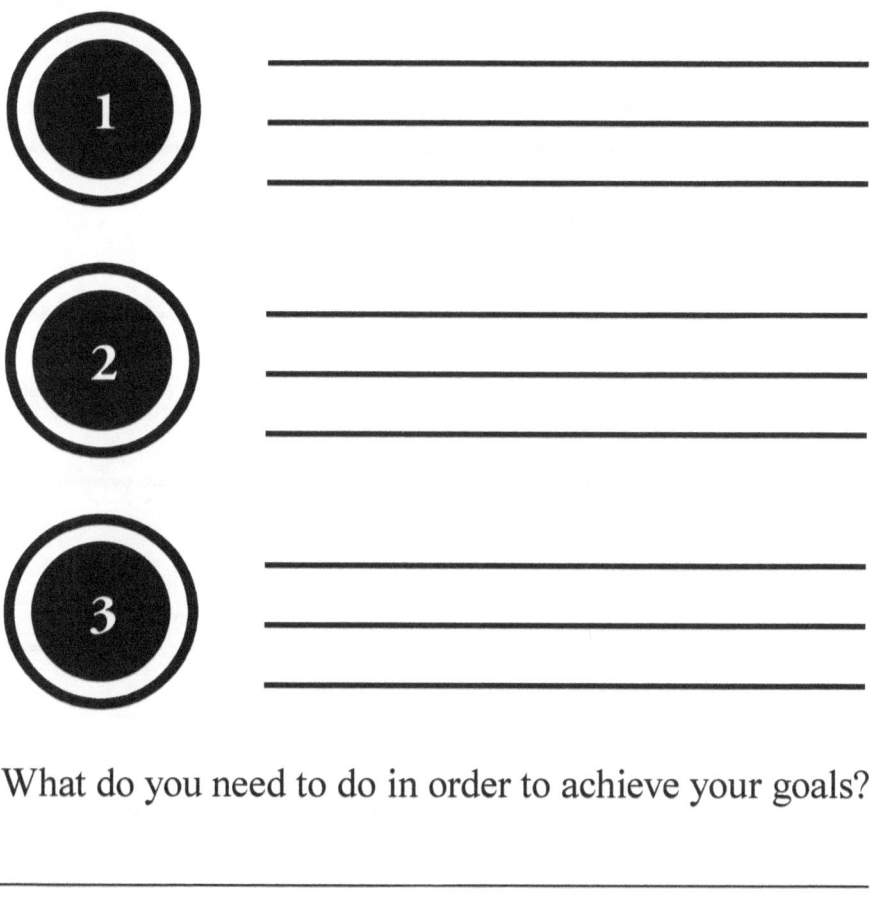

①　_____
　_____
　_____

②　_____
　_____
　_____

③　_____
　_____
　_____

What do you need to do in order to achieve your goals?

_____
_____
_____

Me time: what will you do for *you* this week?

December
2020

December 2020

Su	M	Tu	W	Th	F	Sa
		1	2	3	4	5
6	7	8	9	10	11	12
13	14	15	16	17	18	19
20	21	22	23	24	25	26
27	28	29	30	31		

MON
21

TUE
22

WED
23

THUR
24

FRI
25

SAT
26

SUN
27

Checklist:

☐

_____

☐

_____

☐

_____

☐

_____

☐

_____

☐

Notes:

_____

_____

_____

Reflections

What happened this week, and what did you learn?

Someone somewhere is
living a better life because
of what you have done.

Weekly Goal

List the top 3 goals you want to achieve this week:

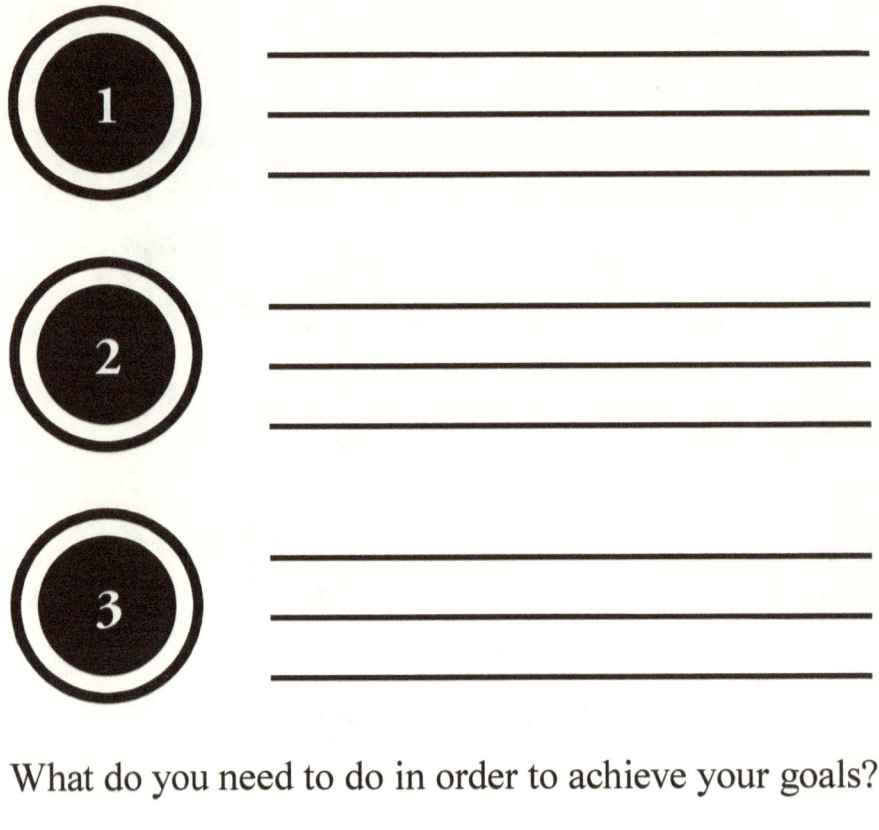

1 _____

_____

_____

2 _____

_____

_____

3 _____

_____

_____

What do you need to do in order to achieve your goals?

_____

_____

_____

Me time: what will you do for _you_ this week?

December
2020

December 2020

Su	M	Tu	W	Th	F	Sa
		1	2	3	4	5
6	7	8	9	10	11	12
13	14	15	16	17	18	19
20	21	22	23	24	25	26
27	28	29	30	31		

MON 28	
TUE 29	
WED 30	
THUR 31	
FRI 01	
SAT 02	
SUN 03	

269

Checklist:

☐

☐

☐

☐

☐

☐

Notes:

Reflections

What happened this week, and what did you learn?

Supervision

How do you want to utilize your supervision session today?

Agenda

Feedback/Advice

Supervision

How do you want to utilize your supervision session today?

Agenda

Feedback/Advice

Supervision

How do you want to utilize your supervision session today?

```
┌─────────────────────────────────────┐
│              Agenda                  │
│                                      │
│                                      │
│                                      │
│                                      │
│                                      │
│                                      │
│                                      │
└─────────────────────────────────────┘
```

```
┌─────────────────────────────────────┐
│           Feedback/Advice            │
│                                      │
│                                      │
│                                      │
│                                      │
│                                      │
│                                      │
│                                      │
└─────────────────────────────────────┘
```

Supervision

How do you want to utilize your supervision session today?

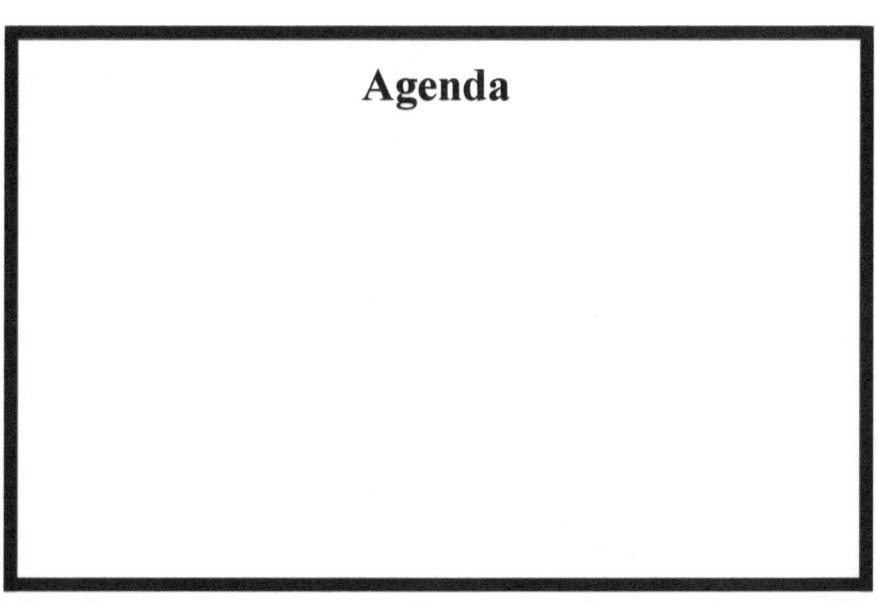

Supervision

How do you want to utilize your supervision session today?

Agenda

Feedback/Advice

Supervision

How do you want to utilize your supervision session today?

```
┌─────────────────────────────────────┐
│              Agenda                  │
│                                      │
│                                      │
│                                      │
│                                      │
│                                      │
│                                      │
└─────────────────────────────────────┘
```

```
┌─────────────────────────────────────┐
│           Feedback/Advice            │
│                                      │
│                                      │
│                                      │
│                                      │
│                                      │
│                                      │
└─────────────────────────────────────┘
```

Supervision

How do you want to utilize your supervision session today?

Agenda

Feedback/Advice

Supervision

How do you want to utilize your supervision session today?

Agenda

Feedback/Advice

Supervision

How do you want to utilize your supervision session today?

Agenda

Feedback/Advice

Supervision

How do you want to utilize your supervision session today?

Agenda

Feedback/Advice

Supervision

How do you want to utilize your supervision session today?

Agenda

Feedback/Advice

Supervision

How do you want to utilize your supervision session today?

Agenda

Feedback/Advice

Continued Professional Development

Date:

Tutor/Trainor or Author:

Title of course/book or article:

Continued Professional Development

Date:

Tutor/Trainor or Author:

Title of course/book or article:

Continued Professional Development

Date:

Tutor/Trainor or Author:

Title of course/book or article:

Continued Professional Development

Date:

Tutor/Trainor or Author:

Title of course/book or article:

Continued Professional Development

Date:

Tutor/Trainor or Author:

Title of course/book or article:

Continued Professional Development

Date:

Tutor/Trainor or Author:

Title of course/book or article:

Continued Professional Development

Date:

Tutor/Trainor or Author:

Title of course/book or article:

Continued Professional Development

Date:

Tutor/Trainor or Author:

Title of course/book or article:

Continued Professional Development

Date:

Tutor/Trainor or Author:

Title of course/book or article:

Continued Professional Development

Date:

Tutor/Trainor or Author:

Title of course/book or article:

Continued Professional Development

Date:

Tutor/Trainor or Author:

Title of course/book or article:

Continued Professional Development

Date:

Tutor/Trainor or Author:

Title of course/book or article: